Food for Tots

Food for Tots

The complete guide to feeding preschoolers, including 100+ kid-tested recipes

Dr. Janice Woolley, Pediatrician
& Jennifer Pugmire, Mom

FOOD FOR TOTS PUBLISHING, DIVISION OF MAMMOTH MEDIA

Food for Tots

The Complete Guide to Feeding Preschoolers

Food for Tots, Division of Mammoth Media, Inc.
P.O. Box 241
Mercer Island, WA. 98040-0241
Telephone 1-866-foodfortots
Fax 1-206-374-2864
Email: info@foodfortots.com

ISBN 1-890908-01-0

Printed in the United States of America

Illustrator: Marilyn Taggart

Cover and Interior Design: Peri Poloni, Knockout Design
www.knockoutbooks.com

Editor: MaryJan Munger

Website address: www.foodfortots.com

What Kids Are Saying

"This cookbook is going to be so big it will be as big as the house because it has so many things."

"I love it 1 billion. 'Cause I just love it because I love carrots."

"Food makes my body grow."

"I like to eat them always, for dinner and lunch and snack."

"I always like to help my mom when she's making something like cookies."

"I used to be picky, picky, picky."

What the Reviewers are Saying

"Well written accurate and up-to-date information. Fits my philosophy of feeding kids."

—Nanna Cross, PhD, RD, UW Family Practice, Cheyenne, WY

"You offer very comprehensive, sensible information in a great, easy-to-read format. The book addresses volumes of common concerns parents have! This will be very useful to my clients and I can't wait to review it for Tiny Tummies!"

—Sanna James Delmonico, MS, RD, Editor, Tiny Tummies Nutrition News, www.TinyTummies.com, Napa, CA

"The chapter on infant feeding is excellent."

—Susan Doyle, RD, Verona, WI

"A great resource for parents. Information about child nutrition, behavioral aspects of feeding children of all ages, and fun recipes to engage toddlers. My patients and their families will benefit from this book."

—Danette S. Glassy, MD, President, Washington Chapter of American Academy of Pediatrics

"I love the format, it's very friendly and would calm a nervous mom. It meets a lot of needs from the young teenage mom to the experienced mom with more than one child. Great guide for other caretakers, grandparents, and dads as well."

—Debra A. Indorato, RD, CPFT, Approach Nutrition and Fitness, Allentown, PA

"Easy enjoyable reading. The First Year chapter is good and very straight forward. Good information on normal toddler behavior and how it translates into eating."

—Roseanne I. Jones, MS, RD, CDN, Cazenovia, NY

"The Eating Behaviors chapter is my favorite. I will recommend this to many friends, family, and clients. Great information and well presented!"

—Annette Lakes, MEd, RD, LD, Cincinnati, OH

"This book contains an amazing number of very practical suggestions to help parents encourage healthy eating behaviors in their young children."

—K. Kim Lampson Reiff, PhD, Eating Disorders Therapist, Mercer Island, WA

"Healthy eating and young children–often these two don't mix. But, Food for Tots not only mixes the two–it does it deliciously! One of the best gifts we can give our children and grandchildren is healthy eating habits to last them a lifetime and this book is filled with appealing recipes to help you do just that."

—JoAnna M. Lund, Cookbook Author and Newsletter Publisher, *Cooking Healthy with the Kids in Mind; Make a Joyful Table; The Healthy Exchanges Cookbook* www.healthyexchanges.com

"Great book! Covers all the bases."

—Beth Zupec-Kania, RD, CD, Children's Hospital of WI

This book is dedicated

to parents, teachers, grandparents,

and other caregivers of those children

who will put anything but

food into their mouths.

Table of Contents

Preface x
Acknowledgements xii

Recipes

Beverages—Yummy sips for little lips 17
Breakfast—Start the day right by filling tummies with good nutrition . . 27
Lunch—Take a break for a quick and healthy lunch 45
Dinner—You'll love these child-friendly family dinners 59
Snacks—Healthy homemade snacks for nibblers 79
Desserts—Sweet treats for little sweethearts 93
Little Helpers—Hands-on experience for budding chefs 109
Special Times—Great ideas for holidays and birthdays 129
Food for Play—Kitchen fun with common ingredients 151

Nutrition

Feeding Baby—What to feed in that important first year 167
Nutrition for Your Growing Child—Baby food to family meals 183
Eating Behaviors—How to handle common feeding problems 203
Food and Health—Food allergies, food safety, feeding sick kids 235

Growth Charts 259
Resources 274
Index 280

Preface

Some young children seem to be like the little ferns that draw nutrition from the air. When you watch them eat you can't help but wonder how they are getting enough to actually grow and thrive. Why is it that sometimes it seems they will put anything but food into their mouths? What is a parent to do? We have written this book to help. We have found out what works and are passing it on to you. Our goal is to uncomplicate the task of feeding your young child and to help you have fun in the process.

In the first part of the book we have provided easy, nutritious recipes. You won't find any exotic ingredients or complicated cooking techniques. As moms ourselves, we know how busy you are. Our recipes have been extensively tested on young children. Some are designed to provide sneaky ways to get vegetables and other goodies into picky eaters. There are recipes for every day, for holidays, and for kitchen crafts. You will also find recipes that your child will love to help you prepare. The whole family will enjoy the delicious results!

In the reference section of the book we supply all the nutrition information you need to choose a good diet for your child. The feeding and nutrition advice is based on sound scientific information and on years of advising parents about feeding their young children. In this section there are also practical tips to help you guide your child's developing relationship with food and eating. Establishing healthy attitudes now can help prevent future eating disorders. In addition, you will find here what you need to know about food allergy, food poisoning, how to prevent choking, and what to feed your child when he is sick.

So, even if you have the world's pickiest eater at your table, there is hope! Writing this book for you has been a great adventure, we hope you benefit from our efforts to help you in your very important job of nurturing your young child.

Best Wishes,

Janice Woolley, Pediatrician

Jennifer Pugmire, Mom

Please Note

The information contained in this book is for informational purposes only and is not intended to substitute for the advice of your child's pediatrician. If you have concerns about your child's health or nutrition you should consult your child's physician. Never disregard professional medical advice or delay seeking it because of something you have read in this book. If at any time you think you may have a medical emergency, call your doctor or 911 immediately.

The information in this book is as accurate as possible, but may contain errors or omissions. Some material might be outdated at the time you read it. The authors and publisher have no legal responsibility or liability for errors, omissions, out-of-date material, or the reader's use of the advice or recipes contained in this book.

It is the responsibility of the caregiver to determine what food is offered to a child and to provide supervision while the child is eating. The caregiver is also responsible for deciding what kitchen activities are appropriate and safe for a child and for providing supervision during those activities.

Thanks to:

Our husbands Jack and Jon, for love, encouragement, many hours of computer support, and for keeping the little ones happy while we wrote.

Norma Whitehead, mother, grandmother, and great-grandmother, who started a tradition of good cooking and healthy eating.

Our children, who provided us with practical experience and ideas.

The preschoolers, ours and others, who taste-tested, helped cook, and posed for pictures.

Babysitters, especially Kim Downing, Bailey Mortensen, Stephanie Davis, and Patrice Dean.

Friends who helped in many ways, Melissa Clayton, Ann Fredrickson, June Griffin, Erika Knudsen, Maureen McConnell, Andrea Mortensen, Karen Seaman, and Antonia Watkins.

Marilyn Taggart, artist and illustrator, who added personality and warmth to our words.

Jack and Jim Woolley of Mammoth Sites for a great website design and children's photographs.

Peri Poloni of Knockout Design who designed a perfect cover and book layout and patiently put up with our delays.

MaryJan Munger, editor, for cleaning up our act.

Bob Smith, for guiding us through the printing maze.

The following experts who reviewed parts of the manuscript and provided suggestions. While we used many of their ideas the final manuscript reflects the views of the authors alone.

Joanne Berardi, RD, Children's Hospital Home Care, Children's Hospital of Philadelphia, Philadelphia, PA

Marilou Brodie, MS, RD, CSP, LD, Pediatric Nutrition Consultant, Arkansas Dept of Health, Little Rock, AR

Nanna Cross, PhD, RD, UW Family Practice, Cheyenne, WY

Tanja Cutting, MS, RD, Children's Eating Lab, Scottsdale, AZ

Sanna James Delmonico, MS, RD, Editor, Tiny Tummies Nutrition News, http:www.TinyTummies.com

Susan Doyle, RD, Verona, WI

Dierdre Ellard, MS, RD, CNSD, Brigham and Women's Hospital, Boston, MA

Julie Ellner, MD, Pediatrician, Mercer Island, WA

Danette S. Glassy, MD, President of Washington chapter of American Academy of Pediatrics, Mercer Island, WA

Debra A. Indorato, RD, CPFT, Approach Nutrition and Fitness, Allentown, Pa

Roseanne I. Jones, MS, RD, CDN, Cazenovia, NY

Annette Lakes, MEd, RD, LD, Cincinnati, OH

K. Kim Lampson Reiff, PhD, Eating Disorders Therapist, Mercer Island, WA

Juanita McElwain, MS, RD, LD, Clinical Nutrition Specialist, The Children's Hospital of Alabama, Birmingham, AL

Ramona Maughan Smith, MS, RD, CSP, Federal Way, WA

Ashley Winton, MS, RD, LDN, Hickory, NC

Beth Zupec-Kania, RD, CD, Children's Hospital of WI, Milwaukee, WI

Explanation of Symbols

In the margins of the Recipe section of this book you will see symbols that call your attention to special information about a recipe.

tot tips:

tips on how to involve your child in preparing a recipe, or how to make the recipe more tot-friendly

cook's tips:

notes about preparation techniques

variations:

changes in the recipe to incorporate different ingredients

tot quotes:

comments preschoolers have made about a recipe

Section 1

Recipes

Chapter 1

Beverages

Yummy sips for little lips

Since babies are used to having liquid meals, it's easy to introduce new flavors in beverages.

Toddlers who are picky eaters will try things in a beverage that they would reject as a solid. Try offering your toddler a nutritious fruit and yogurt smoothie with a muffin for a quick breakfast. Smoothies are easy to make and older children like them, too. If your child is not interested in drinking milk, Orange Banana Milk might be a good way to slip some calcium into the diet at snack time or lunch. For a special occasion, try our Fizzy Fruit Cooler instead of soda pop.

If you like our recipes, try experimenting a little on your own with substitutions of other fresh, frozen, or canned fruits. You can alter the temperature of a drink by substituting water for ice or fresh fruit for frozen fruit. For extra calcium, try adding a spoonful of powdered milk. For a fiber boost, add wheat germ.

Beverage Recipes

1. Orange Banana Milk
2. Grape Milk
3. Fizzy Fruit Juice
4. Tummy Warming Cider
5. Fruity Juice
6. Orange Cooler
7. Strawberry Lemonade
8. Peanut Butter Banana Smoothie
9. Tutti-Frutti Smoothie
10. Cherry Banana Smoothie
11. Easy Piña Colada
12. White Grape & Carrot Juice

Orange Banana Milk

This milk is packed with nutrition! It is a great way to sneak fruit into a picky toddler's diet or to disguise milk.

1 2/3 cups milk

1/3 cup (3 ounces) frozen orange juice concentrate

1/2 medium banana

1 tablespoon wheat germ (optional)

1. Place all ingredients in blender.
2. Cover and blend until foamy.
3. Serve immediately or the banana will cause drink to turn brown.

Yield: 3 cups

Grape Milk

A yummy variation on Orange Banana Milk.

1 cup milk

3 tablespoons frozen grape juice concentrate

1. Place all ingredients in blender.
2. Cover and blend until foamy.

Yield: 1 1/2 cups

cook's tip:

This is a good way to use bananas that are getting a little too ripe.

tot tip:

For a quick and nutritious breakfast, serve either of these drinks with a muffin, bagel, or toast.

tot tip:

Older toddlers can help measure and stir the juice.

Fizzy Fruit Juice

On special occasions, serve this instead of pop.

1 cup orange juice, cranberry juice, grape juice, apricot nectar, or apple juice

1 cup lemon-lime soda or sparkling water

1. In a small container, combine juice and soda.
2. Pour over ice.

Yield: 2 cups

Tummy Warming Cider

Perfect for a cold winter day.

2 cups apple juice

1 cup orange juice

1/16 teaspoon nutmeg

1/16 teaspoon cinnamon

1. In a small saucepan, mix all ingredients
2. Simmer over low heat for at least 10 minutes.
3. Serve warm.

Yield: 3 cups

Fruity Juice

This cool and refreshing drink is great on a warm summer day.

1 cup chilled pineapple juice

1 cup frozen peaches (about 1/2 of a medium peach)

1. Place all ingredients in blender.
2. Cover and blend until smooth.

Yield: 1 2/3 cups

variations:

Try any combination of fresh or frozen fruit and juice.

Orange Cooler

A homemade version of an Orange Julius.

1/2 cup milk

1/2 cup water

1/3 cup (3 ounces) frozen orange juice concentrate

1/3 cup crushed ice or 2 ice cubes

1 tablespoon sugar

1 teaspoon vanilla

1. Place all ingredients in blender.
2. Cover and blend until no ice chunks remain.

Yield: 2 1/2 cups

tot quote:

"I used to be picky, picky, picky."

Strawberry Lemonade

A fun variation on a classic summer drink.

2/3 cup frozen or fresh strawberries

1 cup lemonade

1. Place all ingredients in blender.
2. Cover and blend until smooth.

Yield: 1 1/2 cups

cook's tip:

Just the milk, banana, and vanilla make a great milk-shake too!

Peanut Butter Banana Smoothie

This drink is not only packed with protein but it tastes great, too.

1 frozen banana

3/4 cup milk

2 tablespoons peanut butter

1/3 cup crushed ice or 2 ice cubes

1/8 teaspoon vanilla

1. Place all ingredients in blender.
2. Cover and blend until smooth.
3. Serve immediately or the banana will cause drink to turn brown.

Yield: 2 cups

Tutti-Frutti Smoothie

A fun blend of fruit and yogurt that is also rich in fiber and vitamins.

1/2 orange, peeled & sectioned
1 cup frozen strawberries
1/2 cup apricot nectar
1/3 cup plain yogurt
2-3 teaspoons sugar

1. Place orange sections, strawberries, apricot nectar, and yogurt in a blender.
2. Cover and blend until smooth.
3. Add sugar to taste.

Yield: 1 3/4 cups

tot tip:

Use regular yogurt for children under two. After age two you can use lowfat or nonfat yogurt.

cook's tip:

Don't use yogurt with artificial sweeteners. The flavor will not be as good.

Cherry Banana Smoothie

Try this instead of a milkshake for a delicious treat!

1 container (6–8 ounces) cherry yogurt

1/2 frozen banana

1/4 cup milk

2/3 cup crushed ice or 4 ice cubes

1. Place all ingredients in blender.
2. Cover and blend until smooth.

Yield: 2 cups

Easy Piña Colada

Kids and adults are sure to love this creamy, high-calcium drink.

1 container (6–8 ounces) piña colada yogurt, frozen

1 cup pineapple juice

1/4 cup milk

1. Run hot water over frozen carton of yogurt to loosen contents.
2. Dump yogurt into blender.
3. Add pineapple juice and milk.
4. Cover and blend until smooth.

Yield: 2 1/2 cups

White Grape & Carrot Juice

Save money by making this juice at home for your baby.

1 cup white grape juice
3 tablespoons baby food carrots

1. Place all ingredients in blender.
2. Cover and blend until well mixed.

Yield: 1 cup

variations:

Substitute strained sweet potato or any strained fruit.

Other Beverage Ideas

- Add a banana when mixing frozen orange juice and puree the juice in blender until smooth.
- Freeze juice into ice cubes to put in drinks or to make slushes.
- Have ripe bananas that need to be used? Freeze peeled bananas in resealable freezer bags and use later in blender drinks.
- Freeze berries by putting one layer of washed fruit on a baking sheet lined with waxed paper. Freeze until solid, and put fruit in resealable freezer bags. Enjoy smoothies all year long.
- Don't forget to offer water to your child in between meals.
- Consider ordering milk or milk shakes at restaurants instead of carbonated drinks, which have no real nutrition.
- Don't give caffeinated soft drinks to preschoolers.
- **Never** give a young child unpasteurized juice.
- When you buy boxed drinks for your child choose those that are 100% juice without food colorings or added sugars.
- Limit preschoolers to no more than six ounces of juice a day.
- Never put a baby or child to bed with a juice or milk bottle.

Chapter 2

Breakfast

Start the day right by filling tummies with good nutrition

Breakfast is the most important meal of the day. Young children are often hungriest in the morning so it can be a good time to get some nutritious food into your little one. Research has shown that children who eat a good breakfast learn better and behave better throughout the day than those who skimp on breakfast.

If mornings are rushed, stock your pantry with a good supply of healthy foods that don't require much preparation. Make muffins ahead of time and freeze them for later. Just serve one of our muffins with a smoothie from the Beverage chapter for a complete and nutritious breakfast. If you're watching your budget try making homemade muesli or oatmeal instead of buying expensive ready-to-eat cereals.

Breakfast Recipes

Breads

1. Donut Muffins
2. Sweet Potato Muffins
3. Prune Muffins
4. Apple Crisp Muffins
5. Peanut Butter, Banana, & Jam Minimuffins
6. Refrigerator Bran Muffins
7. Fruit & Cereal Breakfast Cake
8. Whole Grain Pancakes
9. Muesli

Egg Dishes

1. Make-Ahead Breakfast Casserole
2. Omelets
3. Banana French Toast
4. Crepes
5. Breakfast Burritos

Donut Muffins

Kids love these easy-to-make muffins.
They are a great substitute for fried donuts.

1/2 cup milk
1/3 cup vegetable oil
1/3 cup sugar
1 egg
1 1/2 cups flour
1 1/2 teaspoons baking powder
1/2 teaspoon salt
1/4 teaspoon nutmeg

1. Set oven to 350°.
2. Lightly grease a muffin pan.
3. In a medium bowl mix milk, oil, sugar, and egg.
4. Sift together flour, baking powder, salt, and nutmeg.
5. Combine flour mixture and milk mixture just until moistened. Batter will be lumpy.
6. Fill medium muffin cups 1/2 full, minimuffin cups to the top.
7. Bake for 20–25 minutes for medium muffins, 8–10 minutes for minimuffins, or until tops spring back when lightly touched.

Serving suggestion:

Set out a small bowl of melted butter and one of cinnamon-sugar. Kids love to dip the tops of the warm muffins in butter and then cinnamon-sugar.

Yield: 12 medium muffins or about 24 minimuffins

tot quote:

"They are so good, I want someone to make them the mostest."

variations:

For peach muffins substitute a 6 ounce jar of peach baby food for the sweet potato baby food.

Sweet Potato Muffins

A jar of baby food provides a sneaky vegetable addition to this yummy muffin.

1 cup white flour
3/4 cup whole wheat flour
4 teaspoons baking powder
1/2 teaspoon salt
1/2 teaspoon cinnamon
1/4 teaspoon nutmeg
1/2 cup brown sugar
1 jar (6 ounces) sweet potato baby food
1 egg
2/3 cup milk
1/4 cup vegetable oil

1. Set oven to 400°.
2. Lightly grease a muffin pan.
3. Into a medium bowl sift flours, baking powder, salt, cinnamon, and nutmeg.
4. Stir in brown sugar and then make a well in the center of the mixture.
5. In a separate bowl beat together baby food, egg, milk, and oil until well mixed.
6. Pour baby food mixture into flour well and mix just until moistened. Batter will be lumpy.
7. Fill medium muffin cups 3/4 full, minimuffin cups to the top.
8. Bake for 14–17 minutes for medium muffins, 7–9 minutes for minimuffins, or until tops spring back when lightly touched.

Yield: 12 medium muffins or 36 minimuffins

Prune Muffins

Don't be scared off by the prunes. These moist, fiber-filled muffins have passed toddler taste-tests with flying colors.

1 3/4 cups flour
1/4 cup sugar
1 tablespoon baking powder
1/2 teaspoon salt
1/2 teaspoon cinnamon
2 jars (4 ounces each) prune w/ apple baby food
1 egg
1/3 cup milk
1/4 cup vegetable oil

Topping:
2 tablespoons wheat germ
1 tablespoon sugar
1/2 teaspoon cinnamon

1. Set oven to 400°.
2. Lightly grease a muffin pan.
3. Into a medium bowl sift flour, sugar, baking powder, salt, and cinnamon. Make a well in the center.
4. In a separate bowl beat together baby food, egg, milk, and oil with a fork.
5. Pour baby food mixture into flour well and mix just until moistened. Batter will be lumpy.
6. Fill medium muffin cups 3/4 full, minimuffin cups to the top.
7. Combine topping ingredients, sprinkle onto muffins and gently pat on.
8. Bake 14–17 minutes for medium muffins, 7–9 minutes for minimuffins or until tops spring back when lightly touched.

Yield: 12 medium muffins or 36 minimuffins

tot tip:

Baking muffins in a minimuffin pan makes them the perfect size for little hands and there is less waste too!

Apple Crisp Muffins

These low-fat and nutritious muffins are always a hit with the toddler crowd!

1 1/4 cups flour
3/4 cup quick-cooking oats
1/2 cup brown sugar
1 tablespoon baking powder
1 teaspoon cinnamon
1/2 teaspoon salt
1 cup milk
3/4 cup applesauce
1 egg
2 tablespoons vegetable oil
1 teaspoon vanilla
1 1/2 cups peeled diced apples (2 medium apples)

Topping:
1/3 cup quick-cooking oats
1/4 cup flour
2 tablespoons brown sugar
2 tablespoons butter, melted

1. Set oven to 375°.
2. Lightly grease a muffin pan.
3. In a medium bowl combine flour, oats, brown sugar, baking powder, cinnamon, and salt.
4. In a separate bowl whisk together milk, applesauce, egg, oil, and vanilla.
5. Stir milk mixture into flour mixture until just moistened. Stir in diced apples.

6. Fill medium muffin cups 3/4 full, minimuffin cups to the top.
7. Combine topping ingredients until crumbly and sprinkle over muffins.
8. Bake 16–18 minutes for medium muffins, 10–12 minutes for minimuffins or until tops spring back when lightly touched.

Yield: 12 medium muffins or 36 minimuffins

tot quote:

"These taste like cookies."

tot tip:

Children can help by spooning jam into the center of muffins.

Peanut Butter, Banana, & Jam Minimuffins

Just the right size for little hands, and loaded with nutritious ingredients.

1/2 cup peanut butter
1/2 cup mashed banana (about 1 large banana)
1/2 cup milk
1/3 cup brown sugar
1 egg
1 teaspoon vanilla
3/4 cup flour
1/2 tablespoon baking powder
1 cup oats
1/4 cup wheat germ
1/3–1/2 cup jam, any flavor

1. Set oven to 375°.
2. Lightly grease a minimuffin pan.
3. In a medium bowl mix peanut butter, banana, milk, brown sugar, egg, and vanilla.
4. Sift together flour and baking powder and stir into peanut butter mixture.
5. Add oats and wheat germ and mix until combined.
6. Fill minimuffin cups to the top and spoon a little jam into the center top of each muffin.
7. Bake for 10–12 minutes or until edges are golden brown.

Yield: 36 minimuffins

Refrigerator Bran Muffins

This batter can be kept in a tightly covered container in the refrigerator for up to two weeks. You can bake a few at a time, as you need them.

3 cups All Bran or similar cereal
2 cups boiling water
4 eggs, slightly beaten
2 cups plain yogurt
1/2 cup vegetable oil
2 1/2 cups whole wheat flour
2/3 cup sugar
4 teaspoons baking soda
1/2 teaspoon salt

1. Set oven to 400°.
2. Lightly grease a muffin pan.
3. Pour bran cereal into a large bowl. Stir in boiling water, mixing thoroughly. Set aside to cool.
4. Add eggs, yogurt, and oil to cooled bran mixture and mix until well blended.
5. Into a separate bowl sift flour, sugar, baking soda, and salt. Stir flour mixture into bran mixture.
6. Fill medium muffin cups 3/4 full, minimuffin cups to the top.
7. Bake for 17–19 minutes for medium muffins, 8–10 minutes for minimuffins or until tops spring back when lightly touched.

Yield: 30–36 medium muffins or 90–100 minimuffins

variations:

Raisins, currants, mixed dried fruit bits, fresh or thawed frozen blueberries, or mashed banana can be added to the batter before baking. Use 1/2 cup fruit for every 2 cups of batter.

cook's tip:

No time to cook breakfast? Bake this the night before.

Fruit & Cereal Breakfast Cake

A perfect start for a busy day. One piece of cake provides something from every food group.

1 cup orange juice
2/3 cup powdered milk
1 1/2 cups raisin bran cereal
1/4 cup vegetable oil
1 egg, lightly beaten
2 small bananas, thinly sliced
1 1/2 cups flour
1/2 cup sugar
1 teaspoon baking soda
1 teaspoon ground cinnamon
1/2 teaspoon salt

1. Set oven to 350°.
2. Lightly grease an 8x8 inch baking pan.
3. In a medium bowl mix orange juice and powdered milk.
4. Stir in raisin bran and let mixture stand until soft, about 2 minutes.
5. Mix in oil, egg, and bananas.
6. Sift flour, sugar, baking soda, cinnamon, and salt into the raisin bran mixture and stir until just moistened. Batter will be lumpy.
7. Spread in pan and bake 40–45 minutes or until top springs back when lightly touched.

Yield: 8x8 inch pan

Whole Grain Pancakes

High fiber, high calcium and delicious too. Hearty enough to serve for dinner.

1 cup plain yogurt
3/4 cup milk
1/2 cup oats
2 eggs, beaten
1 tablespoon vegetable oil
1/2 cup whole wheat flour
1/2 cup white flour
1 teaspoon baking soda
3/4 teaspoon cinnamon
1/2 teaspoon nutmeg
1/4 teaspoon salt

1. In a large mixing bowl mix yogurt and milk. Stir in oats and put aside to soften.
2. Start preheating griddle.
3. Stir eggs and oil into yogurt mixture.
4. Sift flours, soda, cinnamon, nutmeg, and salt into yogurt mixture and stir until well moistened. The batter should be slightly lumpy.
5. When griddle is warm enough that drops of water sprinkled onto it dance, spray it lightly with vegetable cooking spray.
6. Spoon batter onto griddle. 1/4 cup will make a medium to large pancake. For a toddler's serving use 1–2 tablespoons of batter.
7. Cook until pancakes have bubbly surface and slightly dry edges. Turn and cook on the other side until golden brown. If pancakes are browning too quickly reduce heat so centers cook thoroughly.

Yield: 12–14 medium pancakes

variations:

Just before cooking batter stir in 1 cup of coarsely chopped peeled apple or 1 cup blueberries.

tot tip:

Drop batter onto the griddle to make shapes such as bunny or Mickey Mouse faces, letters, or numbers.

variations:

For adults and children over three sunflower seeds, slivered almonds, or coarsely chopped walnuts or pecans may be added.

cook's tip:

Double or triple the recipe and store in a tightly closed container.

Muesli

When baby outgrows formula and infant cereal here is a good way to use up the leftovers. Older children and adults like this healthy cereal and will never guess what is in it.

1 1/2 cups quick cooking oats

3/4 cup infant dry cereal, such as rice or oatmeal (optional)

1/2 cup All Bran or similar cereal

2 scoops infant formula or 1/4 cup powdered milk

1/4 cup brown sugar

1/2 teaspoon cinnamon

1/2 cup mixed dried fruit bits or raisins

1. Place all ingredients into a resealable plastic storage container.
2. Put the lid on securely and shake the container until the cereal is well mixed.

Serving suggestions:

Serve cold with formula, milk, or yogurt. Serve hot by cooking equal amounts of cereal and milk or water in the microwave for 30–45 seconds. Top with sliced fruit or berries.

Yield: 3 1/2 cups

Make-Ahead Breakfast Casserole

Get a head start on your day. Assemble this easy quiche at night and just pop it in the oven the next morning! This is a great recipe to make when you have overnight guests.

4 slices bread, any kind
3/4 pound sausage, cooked & drained
3/4 cup sliced mushrooms
1/2 cup sliced zucchini
1/2 cup chopped tomato
1 cup grated cheddar cheese
6 eggs
2 cups milk
1 teaspoon mustard
1 teaspoon salt
1/8 teaspoon pepper

1. Lightly grease a 9x13 inch casserole dish.
2. Tear bread into small pieces and arrange in the dish.
3. Spoon meat over bread.
4. Arrange vegetables on top of meat and sprinkle cheese over vegetables.
5. In a mixing bowl or blender, beat eggs, milk, mustard, salt, and pepper until frothy. Pour egg mixture over cheese.
6. Cover and refrigerate overnight.
7. In the morning preheat oven to 350° and bake 35–40 minutes or until set.

Yield: 9x13 inch casserole

variations:

Other vegetables such as chopped red or green pepper, onion, or broccoli can be used. Cubed ham can be substituted for the sausage.

tot tip:

Any vegetables that your toddler does not like can be omitted from all or part of the casserole.

tot quote:

"My favorite is the baby hot dogs, that's why I always eat them first."

Omelets

Made-to-order omelets will please even picky toddlers. Mixing the egg with water instead of milk creates a lighter omelet.

1 egg

1 tablespoon water

- ***grated cheese***
- ***ham, smokey links, or other meat, chopped or sliced***
- ***mushrooms, zucchini, onions, or other vegetables, chopped***

1. In a small bowl, beat egg and water with a fork until fluffy.
2. Place a 7–9 inch nonstick pan over medium heat and coat well with vegetable cooking spray or butter.
3. Pour egg mixture into pan. As eggs set, gently lift edges with spatula so uncooked portion can flow underneath.
4. When egg is almost set, sprinkle cheese, meat, and vegetables on one half of omelet. Fold empty half on top of fillings.
5. Cover and cook over low heat until egg is no longer runny.

Yield: 1 child-sized omelet, for an adult serving use 2–3 eggs

Banana French Toast

A sneaky way to get fruit into little tummies.

1 large ripe banana

2 eggs

1/4 cup milk

1/8 teaspoon cinnamon

6 slices whole wheat bread

1. In a shallow dish mash banana with a fork until smooth.
2. Add eggs, milk, and cinnamon and whip with a fork until well blended.
3. Dip both sides of bread in egg mixture.
4. Fry in a buttered pan over medium heat until both sides are light brown and egg is thoroughly cooked.

Yield: 6 slices

cook's tip:

French toast slices can be frozen in single servings, then just popped in the toaster to reheat.

tot tip:

Slice toast into strips for dipping in yogurt, syrup, jam, or applesauce.

cook's tip:

Spray spatula with nonstick spray and crepes will be easy to turn over.

Crepes

Easy-to-make crepes can make any morning seem special.

2 eggs

2 cups milk

1 1/2 tablespoons melted butter

1 cup flour

1 1/2 teaspoons sugar

1/2 teaspoon salt

1. In a medium bowl beat eggs well with a fork.
2. Add milk and butter to eggs.
3. In a separate bowl combine flour, sugar, and salt.
4. Add flour mixture to egg mixture and stir until evenly mixed.
5. Pour onto a hot buttered griddle or crepe pan. Use 1/3 cup for an adult, 1/4 cup for a child.
6. Cook over medium heat until first side is lightly browned then turn and cook other side until set.

Serving suggestions:

Place fresh fruit, yogurt, or jam in the center of each crepe and fold ends over the filling. Garnish with powdered sugar, jam, or syrup.

Yield: 10–12 crepes

Breakfast Burritos

Wrap up breakfast for one or two or for a crowd.

- ***egg(s)***

1 tablespoon milk per egg

- ***chopped ham, smokey links, or other meat***
- ***flour tortilla(s)***
- ***shredded cheese***
- ***chopped tomato or salsa***

1. Scramble eggs with milk in a frying pan, being sure to cook eggs thoroughly.
2. Cook meat.
3. Warm the tortillas.
4. Put cheese, tomato, and salsa into small serving dishes.

Serving suggestions:

Serve buffet style. Everyone can choose what they want and then roll the tortilla up like a burrito.

Yield: varies, for 1 child-sized burrito use 1 egg, for an adult use 2–3 eggs

variations:

Use other condiments if desired, such as sliced olives, mushrooms, peppers, or avocado.

Other Breakfast Ideas

- Peanut butter, jam, and banana sandwich with milk
- Leftover dinner food
- Broiled cheese sandwich with fruit or juice
- **Mac 'n' Cheese**, fruit or juice
- Leftover cooked rice topped with yogurt and fruit
- Bagel with cream cheese, fruit juice
- Homemade english muffin egg and cheese sandwich, **Fruit Leather**, and milk
- Scrambled eggs, whole grain toast, milk, and fruit
- Whole grain toaster waffles or pancakes
- Sausage and bacon are high in fat and sodium and are best used only occasionally.
- Unsugared whole grain cereals topped with fresh, frozen, or dried fruits.

Chapter 3

Lunch

Take a break for a quick and healthy lunch

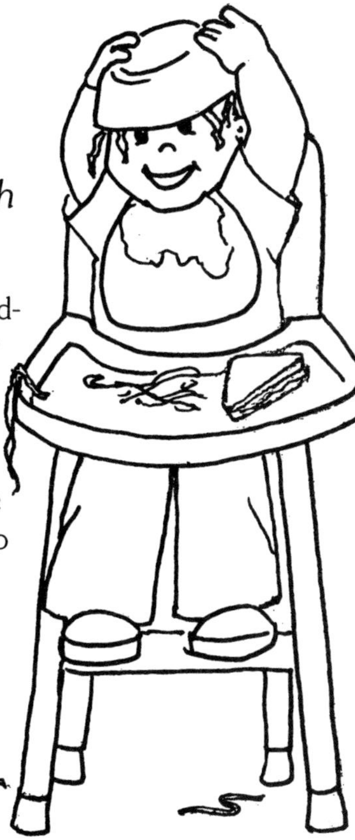

Preschoolers are usually on the go all morning. By the middle of the day they are running out of steam and ready for refueling and rest. When you are at home with your child at lunchtime, take time for a simple lunch. An ideal lunch should contain a dairy product, a grain, a fruit or vegetable, and some protein. Does this sound like a lot? It isn't really. Lunch doesn't have to be elaborate to be nourishing.

Try some of our easy sandwich ideas or for a little lunchtime variety try Zucchini Quesadillas or Tortilla Wraps. Want a hot lunch on a cool day? Mac 'n' Cheese is always a favorite with the preschool set. Instead of the boxed type that is loaded with salt and food coloring try our quick and healthy version.

Who knows—with a full tummy maybe your little one will take a nice long nap!

Lunch Recipes

1. *Tortilla Rollups*
2. *Egg Salad Sandwiches*
3. *Grilled Cheese & Apple Sandwiches*
4. *Zucchini Quesadillas*
5. *English Muffin Pizzas*
6. *Twisty Pasta Salad*
7. *Hawaiian Muffins*
8. *PB & J Mini Pies*
9. *Peek-A-Boo Pockets*
10. *Mac 'n' Cheese*
11. *Tuna Burgers*

Tortilla Rollups

A fun twist on sandwiches. They are easy for little hands to pick up.

- ***flour tortilla(s)***
- ***cream cheese, softened***
- ***lunchmeat or tuna***
- ***cheese (optional)***
- ***thinly sliced tomato***
- ***shredded lettuce***

1. Spread a thin layer of cream cheese over each tortilla.
2. Layer lunchmeat or tuna, cheese, tomato, and lettuce on the tortilla, to within 1/4 inch of the edge.
3. Roll up tortilla, cut into 2–3 pieces and serve.

Yield: varies, make 1/2–1 rollup per child, 1–2 per adult

tot tip:

Let child choose fillings and help make the sandwich.

cook's tip:

Make extra boiled eggs and store them in the fridge for later use. They will store for up to one week.

Egg Salad Sandwiches

A classic lunchtime favorite for all ages.

2 hard-boiled eggs, peeled and chopped

2 tablespoons mayonnaise or salad dressing

1/8 teaspoon dill

1/16 teaspoon salt

- ***dash of curry powder (optional)***

4 slices whole wheat bread

1. Mix together eggs and mayonnaise.
2. Stir in dill, salt, and curry powder.
3. Spread filling onto plain or buttered bread.

Yield: 2 sandwiches

Grilled Cheese & Apple Sandwiches

A yummy variation on an old favorite.

4 slices bread, any kind

- ***butter or margarine***
- ***cheddar cheese, thinly sliced***

1/2 apple, peeled and thinly sliced

- ***cinnamon-sugar***

1. Butter each bread slice and place thin layer of sliced cheese on unbuttered side of two of the bread slices.
2. Place layer of apples on top of cheese and sprinkle with cinnamon sugar.
3. Add one more thin layer of cheese. Top with remaining bread (butter side out).
4. In a medium frying pan, grill sandwich over medium heat until both sides of the bread are golden brown.

Yield: 2 sandwiches

cook's tip:

To make cinnamon-sugar combine 1 1/2 teaspoons sugar & 1/2 teaspoon cinnamon.

cook's tip:

For a faster version, use drained canned chicken, assemble quesadilla and cook in microwave for 30–50 seconds or until cheese melts.

Zucchini Quesadillas

Get some green into their diets by hiding it in these quick and tasty quesadillas.

- ***butter***

2 flour tortillas

- ***cheese such as monterey jack, mozzarella, or cheddar, sliced***
- ***zucchini, thinly sliced***

additional filling options:

- ***chicken, cooked & shredded***
- ***diced tomatoes***
- ***sliced green pepper***
- ***sliced olives***

1. In a frying pan melt a small amount of butter over medium heat.
2. Place 1 tortilla in the pan and cover with thin slices of cheese.
3. Place zucchini and any other fillings over cheese.
4. Put 2nd tortilla on top.
5. Cook until cheese starts to melt and then flip and brown on other side.

Serving suggestions:

Cut like a pie and serve with plain yogurt or sour cream for dipping.

Yield: 1 quesadilla

English Muffin Pizzas

Everyone loves pizza.
Kids can help with this simple version.

1 english muffin
- ***pizza sauce***
- ***grated mozzarella cheese***
- ***ham or chicken, cooked & chopped***
- ***other pizza toppings***

1. Slice english muffin into two halves.
2. Spread pizza sauce on each half.
3. Sprinkle with cheese, meat, and other toppings.
4. Broil until cheese is bubbly.

Yield: 2 small pizzas

variations:

Use minibagels instead of english muffins.

variations:

Substitute macaroni, tortellini, shells, etc. Chicken and marinated artichoke hearts can be used instead of ham for a fancier version.

tot tip:

Keep the ingredients separate and let children choose what they want and mix in their dressing.

Twisty Pasta Salad

This pasta salad makes an ideal summer meal as the only cooking required is the pasta. Add your favorite salad ingredients and some dressing and you're done!

1 package (12 ounces) rainbow rotelle pasta

1 cup cubed ham

1 1/2 cups cubed or grated cheese

3 cups chopped raw vegetables such as:

- ***broccoli***
- ***cucumber***
- ***green or yellow onion***
- ***zucchini squash***
- ***green, yellow, or red peppers***
- ***olives***
- ***bottled salad dressing***

1. Cook pasta according to package directions.
2. In a large serving bowl mix pasta, ham, cheese, and vegetables.
3. Stir in desired amount of your favorite salad dressing. Italian works well.

Yield: 12 cups

Hawaiian Muffins

Served with a glass of milk these make a complete lunch. Make a batch and freeze some for later.

1 1/4 cups flour

1/2 cup corn meal

1/4 cup sugar

1 tablespoon baking powder

1/2 teaspoon salt

2 eggs

1/4 cup vegetable oil

1 cup crushed pineapple with juice (about half of a 20 ounce can)

3/4 cup chopped ham or canadian bacon

1. Set oven to 400°.
2. Lightly grease a muffin pan.
3. Into a medium bowl sift flour, corn meal, sugar, baking powder, and salt. Make a well in the center.
4. In a separate bowl beat together eggs and oil with a fork.
5. Stir pineapple into egg mixture.
6. Pour egg mixture into flour well and mix just until moistened. Batter will be lumpy.
7. Stir in chopped ham or canadian bacon.
8. Fill medium muffin cups 3/4 full, minimuffins to the top.
9. Bake for 15–20 minutes for medium muffins, 10–12 minutes for minimuffins or until tops spring back when lightly touched.

Yield: 12 medium muffins or 36 minimuffins

cook's tip:

Freeze unused pineapple in a resealable plastic freezer bag for later use.

variations:

Substitute roll or bread dough for the refrigerator biscuits.

cook's tip:

Place a cookie sheet in the oven on the shelf below the muffin pan to catch any drips.

PB&J Mini Pies

These are the perfect size for little fingers. They can be made ahead and refrigerated until needed for meals or snacks.

1 package (7 1/2 ounces) refrigerator biscuits
- ***peanut butter***
- ***jam, any kind***

1. Set oven to 400°.
2. Lightly grease a minimuffin pan.
3. Flatten out each biscuit by pressing and stretching gently.
4. Place each flattened biscuit in a minimuffin cup.
5. Put 1/2 teaspoon of peanut butter and 1/2 teaspoon of jam into biscuit and pinch together the top edges of the biscuit.
6. Put a little water into the empty muffin cups before baking.
7. Bake for 8–10 minutes or until lightly browned.

Yield: 10 mini pies

Peek-A-Boo Pockets

These are fun to make and so convenient.
Make extras and freeze them for later use.

18 frozen bread dough rolls, thawed but not raised

1/4 cup pizza sauce

1 cup grated mozzarella cheese

1 cup cooked & chopped ham or chicken

1 cup chopped raw vegetables such as:

- ***tomato***
- ***green peppers***
- ***broccoli***
- ***mushrooms***
- ***olives***

1. Set oven to 375°.
2. Lightly grease a cookie sheet.
3. Flatten 9 of the thawed rolls onto the cookie sheet.
4. Spread 1 teaspoon sauce in the center of each flattened roll.
5. Sprinkle 1–2 tablespoons cheese, meat, and vegetables over sauce.
6. Flatten the remaining rolls, place over bottom rolls, and seal edges with a fork.
7. Bake for 15–18 minutes or until the tops are light brown.

Yield: 9 pocket sandwiches

variations:

Leave out pizza sauce and use canned tuna instead of ham or chicken.

tot quote:

"Food makes my body grow."

variations:

Add garlic powder, grated onion, or pepper for even more flavor.

Mac 'n' Cheese

This home-made version is not only healthier, but better-tasting than the boxed macaroni and cheese. It can also be served for dinner.

2 cups uncooked elbow macaroni (an 8 ounce package)

2 cups milk

2 tablespoons flour

2 tablespoons butter, melted

2 teaspoons mustard

2 cups grated sharp cheddar cheese

1. Cook macaroni according to package directions.
2. In a blender mix milk, flour, and melted butter until thoroughly blended.
3. In a medium saucepan cook milk mixture over low heat, stirring constantly until sauce thickens.
4. Mix mustard into milk mixture then slowly stir in grated cheese until melted.
5. Remove saucepan from heat.
6. In a serving bowl combine pasta and cheese sauce and garnish with grated cheese if desired.

Yield: 4 cups

Tuna Burgers

A flavorful hot sandwich for a quick family supper.

1 can (6 ounces) water-pack tuna, drained
1/2 cup grated cheese
1/3 cup minced celery
1/4 cup minced pickle
1/4 cup minced onion
1/4 cup grated carrot
3 tablespoons mayonnaise or salad dressing
6 buttered hamburger buns

1. Set oven to 350°.
2. Mix tuna, cheese, celery, pickle, onion, carrot, and mayonnaise.
3. Lightly brown hamburger buns under the broiler.
4. Fill buns with tuna mixture and wrap individual sandwiches in tin foil.
5. Heat sandwiches in oven for 15–20 minutes or until cheese melts.

Serving suggestions:

Try these with soup or baked fries.

Yield: 6 sandwiches

cook's tip:

Wear a rubber glove when opening tight jars. You will have better grip.

Other Lunch Ideas

- Tuna salad sandwich with added grated carrot or other vegetables
- Leftover dinner food
- Peanut butter sandwich, milk, and banana slices
- **Chicken Nuggets, Baked Fries,** and **Fizzy Fruit Juice**
- Flour tortilla with melted cheese, apple slices, and milk
- Soup, whole grain crackers, and cubes of cheese
- String cheese, grapes*, whole grain crackers, and water
- Sliced hard boiled egg, buttered whole wheat toast, and **Tutti-Frutti Smoothie**
- Peach or pear half, topped with cottage cheese, and whole grain toast or crackers
- Grilled cheese and turkey sandwich with orange slices and milk
- Cubes of cheese, pretzels or crackers, cut up fresh fruit or fruit juice
- Toast topped with a tomato slice and a slice of cheese—put under broiler to melt cheese

**choking hazard for babies and toddlers*

Chapter 4

Dinner

You'll love these child-friendly dinners

Family dinners are a great time to introduce your child to the foods that you like to eat. While you do have to cater somewhat to young children's tastes and their ability to chew solid foods, you don't always have to cook traditional kid foods such as macaroni and cheese and hot dogs. Your little one will learn to enjoy a variety of foods by being exposed to new foods and watching you enjoy them.

All of our recipes are easy to make and are kid-tested. We also have lots of ideas to help you sneak vegetables into your child's diet. Check out Sneaky Joes, Orange Glazed Carrots, and Easy Cheese Sauce, for example. Or make it easy on yourself by preparing dishes that can be customized to everyone's tastes, such as Chicken Haystacks, Mexican Stackups, and Baked Potato Bar.

Dinner Recipes

Main Dishes

1. *Baked Potato Bar*
2. *Puffy Apple Pancake*
3. *Chicken Nuggets*
4. *Chicken Turtles*
5. *Chicken Haystacks*
6. *Chicken Parmesan*
7. *Mexican Stackups*
8. *Tortilla Bowls*
9. *Mixer Meatloaf*
10. *Sneaky Joes*

Side Dishes

1. *Calico Beans*
2. *Broccoli Salad*
3. *Baked Fries*
4. *Orange Glazed Carrots*
5. *Easy Cheese Sauce*

Baked Potato Bar

Easy, fast, and filling. Provides lots of choices for those hard-to-please little ones.

baking potatoes, 1 per adult, 1/2 per child

Topping options:

- ***butter or margarine***
- ***steamed broccoli***
- ***canned white or black beans, drained & heated***
- ***grated cheese***
- ***chopped tomato***
- ***chopped green onions***
- ***bacon bits***
- ***sour cream***

1. Set oven to 425°.
2. Thoroughly scrub potatoes and prick 3–4 times with a fork. Rub potatoes with oil or shortening for softer skins.
3. Bake potatoes for 40–60 minutes or until a knife inserted in the center easily slides out.
4. Place toppings in serving bowls.

Serving suggestions:

Serve buffet style.

variations:

Use Easy Cheese Sauce in place of grated cheese.

cook's tip:

Potatoes that have been baked in aluminum foil should be kept hot until served, or refrigerated to avoid botulism poisoning.

variations:

Omit the apples, cinnamon, and sugar. After baking, top with one or more of the following: maple or fruit syrup, applesauce, fresh or thawed frozen fruit.

Puffy Apple Pancake

A wonderful light egg soufflé that kids are sure to love! Makes a good meal accompanied by canadian bacon or ham and takes less of the cook's time than regular pancakes.

1/3 cup butter or margarine

2 medium apples

3 tablespoons sugar

2 teaspoons cinnamon

4 eggs

1 cup milk

1 cup flour

- ***powdered sugar (optional)***

1. Set oven to 425°.
2. Put butter into a 9–10 inch frying pan and place in oven until butter is just melted, not browned.
3. While butter is melting, peel and core the apples, then cut them into thin slices.
4. Remove the pan from the oven, add sugar and cinnamon to the melted butter, and stir in the sliced apples.
5. Return pan to oven for about 3 minutes.
6. In a blender whip eggs and milk at high speed for 1 minute. Set the blender to low speed and slowly add the flour until well blended.
7. Remove the pan from the oven and pour egg batter over the butter and apples.
8. Bake for 20–25 minutes or until the pancake is raised and golden brown
9. Serve immediately.

Serving suggestions:

Cut in wedges and dust with powdered sugar.

Yield: 9–10 inch pan

If more servings are desired: for each additional serving, add 1/2 apple, 1 tablespoon sugar, 1 egg, 1/4 cup milk, 1/4 cup flour, and a little more butter and cinnamon.

tot quote:

"I like to eat them always, for dinner and lunch and snack."

tot quote:

"I like 'em!"

Chicken Nuggets

A more nutritious version of the fast food favorite.

2 pounds boneless, skinless chicken breasts (about 2 whole breasts)

• nonstick vegetable oil spray

3/4 cup wheat germ

3/4 cup grated parmesan cheese

1 teaspoon thyme

1 teaspoon basil

1/2 teaspoon salt

1 gallon size resealable plastic bag

1. Set oven to 400°.
2. Lightly spray a cookie sheet with vegetable oil spray.
3. Rinse chicken with cold water, and cut into 1–1 1/2 inch pieces. Pat dry with paper towels.
4. Lightly spray chicken pieces with oil spray so coating will stick.
5. Put wheat germ, cheese, thyme, basil, and salt into plastic bag and shake to mix.
6. Put a few pieces of chicken at a time in bag and shake to coat them.
7. Arrange chicken on cookie sheet and bake for 15–20 minutes. Coating should be lightly browned and chicken cooked through.

Serving suggestions:

Kids like to dip them in barbeque sauce, sweet & sour sauce, or honey.

Yield: 5–6 dozen small nuggets

Chicken Turtles

Kids love the way these look and taste.

1 1/4 cups cooked & chopped chicken (about 1 chicken breast)

4 ounces cream cheese, softened

2 tablespoons milk

1/2 tablespoon chives or onion, chopped

1/8 teaspoon salt

- ***pepper to taste***

3 packages (7 1/2 ounces) refrigerator biscuits (10 in each package)

1. Set oven to 350°.
2. Lightly spray a cookie sheet with vegetable oil spray.
3. In a small bowl combine chicken, cream cheese, milk, chives, salt, and pepper until well mixed.
4. Form the bottom shells for 12 turtles by flattening 12 biscuits onto a cookie sheet.
5. Put a spoonful of chicken mixture in the center of each flattened biscuit. (Use all of the chicken mixture.)
6. Cut 6 of the remaining biscuits into halves. Using 1/2 biscuit for each turtle, form the heads, legs, and tails and position them on the bottom shells. Press them down gently to keep them in place.
7. Form the top shells by flattening the remaining 12 biscuts and placing one on top of each of the turtle bottoms.
8. Press edges together to seal.
9. Cook 16–18 minutes or until tops start to brown.

Yield: 12 turtles

variations:

Use croissant or roll dough. Try canned chicken for convenience.

cook's tip:

The chicken-cream cheese mixture makes a great sandwich spread for bagels and pitas.

Chicken Haystacks

Make-it-your-own-way chicken sundaes are a great dinner for children.

1 can (12 1/2 ounces) chicken, undrained

1 can (10 3/4 ounces) cream of chicken soup

4 cups cooked rice

Topping options:

- ***chow mein noodles***
- ***canned crushed pineapple, drained***
- ***grated cheese***
- ***chopped green onions***
- ***chopped green, yellow, or red peppers***
- ***chopped celery***
- ***shredded coconut***
- ***raisins***
- ***slivered almonds or chopped peanuts***
- ***sweet and sour sauce***
- ***soy sauce***
- ***peanut sauce***

1. In a crockpot, microwave-safe bowl, or pan mix chicken and cream of chicken soup.
2. Cook chicken mixture until heated throughout.
3. Place chicken mixture, rice, and toppings in separate serving bowls.

Serving suggestions:

Serve buffet style. To make sundaes start with a scoop of rice, spoon chicken mixture over the rice, and add desired toppings.

Yield: serves 2 adults & 2 children

variations:

The cream of chicken soup can be served separately from the chicken or can be omitted.

tot tip:

Don't serve nuts to children under three.

Chicken Parmesan

This fast main dish has an Italian touch. Pair it with salad and garlic bread for a complete meal.

3 boneless, skinless chicken breast halves (1 1/2 pounds)

- ***nonstick vegetable oil spray***

1/3 cup italian bread crumbs

2 tablespoons parmesan cheese

2 tablespoons butter or margarine

1 1/2 cups spaghetti sauce

2 tablespoons water

1/2 cup shredded mozzarella cheese

1. Flatten chicken breasts to even thickness with palm of hand.
2. Lightly spray chicken breast halves with oil spray.
3. In a shallow dish combine bread crumbs and 1 tablespoon parmesan cheese.
4. Dip chicken breasts in bread mixture and turn to coat on both sides.
5. In a large frying pan melt butter over medium heat. Add chicken and brown on both sides.
6. Pour sauce and water over chicken and lift chicken up so sauce runs under chicken.
7. Turn heat to low, cover, and cook for 10 minutes.
8. Sprinkle mozzarella cheese and remaining 1 tablespoon parmesan cheese over chicken breasts. Cover and cook for 5 more minutes or until chicken is cooked throughout.

Serving suggestions:

Serve over cooked pasta, egg noodles work well.

Yield: serves 2 adults & 2 children

cook's tip:

Be sure to cook chicken thoroughly to avoid salmonella food poisoning.

cook's tip:

Be sure to cook hamburger thoroughly to avoid food poisoning.

Mexican Stackups

Another way to please picky eaters. Let them pile their choices into a tortilla bowl and eat it, bowl and all.

1 can (16 ounces) refried beans, heated
1 pound hamburger, cooked
1 1/2 cups cooked rice (optional)
1/2 head of lettuce, chopped
4 Tortilla Bowls or tortillas

Topping Options:

- ***grated cheddar cheese***
- ***avocado slices or guacamole***
- ***chopped tomato***
- ***chopped onion***
- ***sliced black olives***
- ***salsa***
- ***sour cream***

1. Make tortilla bowls or warm tortillas.
2. Place all ingredients in separate serving bowls.

Serving suggestions:

Serve buffet style. Put layers of refried beans, hamburger, rice, and lettuce into bowls or on top of tortillas. Add any of the other topping options.

Yield: serves 2 adults & 2 children

Tortilla Bowls

Make salads, fruit, or ice cream more fun by serving them in these eatable bowls.

1 flour tortilla (7 inch)

- ***vegetable oil***

1. Brush one side of the tortilla with oil.
2. Press the tortilla, oil side up, into a microwavable bowl.
3. Microwave on 50% power for 2 minutes.
4. Cook on full power for 20–60 seconds or until tortilla is crisp. Check often, as overcooking will turn the tortilla brown.

Yield: 1 child-sized tortilla bowl, for an adult serving use a 10 inch tortilla

cook's tip:

For a 10 inch tortilla, microwave on 50% power for 2 minutes, and full power for 1–3 minutes.

cook's tip:

Cut leftover meatloaf into pieces and reheat in crockpot with bottled spaghetti sauce for a second meal.

If you don't have a heavy-duty stand mixer, mix this by hand.

Mixer Meatloaf

Save time and avoid mess by using a heavy-duty stand mixer to prepare this meatloaf. The result is moist and delicious and easy for young toddlers to handle.

1 egg
1/4 cup tomato puree
1 jar (4 ounces) mixed vegetable baby food
2 slices whole wheat bread
1 1/2 tablespoons chopped onion
1 1/2 teaspoons worcestershire sauce
1/2 teaspoon salt
1/4 teaspoon pepper
1 pound extra lean hamburger

Sauce:
1/4 cup catsup
2 tablespoons brown sugar
2 teaspoons mustard
1/4 teaspoon nutmeg

1. Set oven to 350°.
2. In electric mixer bowl, beat egg until frothy.
3. Set mixer to low speed and add tomato puree and vegetable baby food.
4. Tear bread into pieces and drop into bowl, mixing until moistened.
5. Mix in onion, worcestershire sauce, salt, and pepper.

6. Slowly add hamburger until blended in and then shape and put into an ungreased loaf pan.
7. Put pan in oven and bake for 1 hour.
8. Mix catsup, brown sugar, mustard, and nutmeg in a small bowl. Spread sauce over meatloaf and bake for 15 more minutes.

Serving suggestions:

Slice and serve with baked potatoes, a vegetable, and bread for a complete meal.

Yield: 1 medium loaf pan

cook's tip:

Leftover filling freezes well and can be reheated in the microwave for a quick meal.

Sneaky Joes

Here's our version of Sloppy Joes, a sneaky way to get vegetables into those reluctant eaters.

1 cup bottled barbecue sauce

1 1/2 cups frozen mixed vegetables

1 1/2 pounds lean ground beef, chicken, or turkey

1 small onion, chopped

6 hamburger buns

1. Put barbecue sauce into a blender or food processor.
2. Add mixed vegetables a little at a time and blend until smooth.
3. In a frying pan cook meat and onion over medium heat until partially done.
4. Stir in sauce mixture, cover the pan and simmer over medium heat, stirring frequently until meat is thoroughly done.
5. While meat simmers, butter the hamburger buns and toast them lightly under the broiler.
6. Spoon meat mixture into buns and serve.

Serving suggestions:

Try these with Baked Fries.

Yield: 6 sandwiches

Calico Beans

A good dish to take to a picnic or a potluck dinner. Serve with raw or lightly steamed vegetable sticks and a dip for a complete meal.

1/4 pound bacon (4–5 slices)
1/2 cup chopped onion
1 large can (31 ounces) pork & beans, drained
1 can (15 ounces) black beans, drained
1 can (15 ounces) white beans, drained
1/2 cup crushed pineapple, drained
1/4 cup chopped green pepper
1/2 cup ketchup
1/4 cup brown sugar
1 tablespoon cider vinegar
1 teaspoon mustard

1. Set oven to 325°.
2. Fry bacon, drain off grease, and chop or tear into bite-sized pieces.
3. Cook onion in a small amount of bacon grease until turning golden in color.
4. Pour all three cans of beans into a 9x13 inch casserole dish.
5. Add bacon, onion, pineapple, and green pepper to beans.
6. In a small bowl mix together ketchup, brown sugar, vinegar, and mustard.
7. Stir ketchup mixture into bean mixture.
8. Bake for 40–50 minutes or until juices bubble.

Yield: 9x13 inch casserole

variations:

Substitute other varieties of beans such as kidney beans, lima beans, or garbanzos.

Broccoli Salad

A delicious fresh tasting salad. Make just the amount your family will eat as it does not keep well.

2 cups (10 ounce package) of frozen chopped broccoli, thawed

1/2 cup chopped onion

1 1/2 cups chopped tomato (1–2 medium sized tomatoes)

1/4 teaspoon of garlic salt

2 tablespoons salad dressing or mayonnaise

1. Pat broccoli dry with a paper towel.
2. Chop up larger stem pieces of broccoli.
3. Mix all ingredients and serve within an hour.

Yield: 4 cups

Baked Fries

Low-fat french fries will please the preschool crowd.

- ***nonstick vegetable oil spray***

1 egg white

1/4 teaspoon paprika

1/4 teaspoon salt

5 cups thinly cut potatoes (about 4 medium potatoes)

1. Set oven to 425°.
2. Cover a cookie sheet with foil and generously spray foil with vegetable oil spray.
3. In a medium bowl beat 1 egg white with a fork until frothy.
4. Add paprika and salt.
5. Add potatoes and stir until coated with egg white mixture.
6. Spread potatoes on cookie sheet.
7. Bake for 20 minutes. Turn fries with spatula and bake for another 10–20 minutes or until golden brown.

Yield: 5 cups

variations:

Try sweet potatoes for a vitamin-rich version.

tot tip:

Omit egg white to make a softer version for children under two years of age.

Orange Glazed Carrots

These lightly sweetened carrots are a good source of vitamin A.

4 cups frozen sliced carrots or about 5–6 fresh carrots, peeled and sliced

2 tablespoons brown sugar

1 teaspoon cornstarch

1/4 teaspoon salt

3 tablespoons orange juice

2 tablespoons butter or margarine

1. Cook carrots by steaming, simmering, or microwaving.
2. Stir together brown sugar, cornstarch, and salt.
3. Mix orange juice into sugar mixture.
4. Add butter to sugar mixture.
5. Cook sauce on stovetop over medium heat stirring until sugar dissolves, or microwave for 1–2 minutes.
6. Pour sauce over carrots and reheat on stovetop or in microwave oven.

Yield: 4 cups

Easy Cheese Sauce

This is just what you need to dress up vegetables for company or to entice little ones to eat their veggies.

1 cup milk

2 tablespoons flour

2 tablespoons margarine

1 cup grated medium cheddar cheese

1. In blender or food processor blend milk, flour, and margarine until smooth.
2. Pour mixture into a saucepan.
3. Cook over medium heat stirring constantly until sauce thickens and bubbles.
4. Turn heat to low and stir in grated cheese until well blended.
5. Cook until cheese is melted.

Serving suggestions:

Serve warm over cooked vegetables or chilled as a dip for raw vegetables.

Yield: 1 1/4 cups

variations:

This is a very mild flavored sauce. If you want more flavor use sharp cheddar cheese or add 1 teaspoon of mustard.

tot quote:

"I like this the same as cake."

Other Dinner Ideas

- Pizza, raw vegetable sticks, and **Fizzy Fruit Cooler**
- Roasted chicken from grocery store, dinner rolls, vegetables with **Cheese Sauce**, fruit, and milk
- Pasta with bottled sauce, topped with grated cheese, raw vegetable sticks, **Dilly Dip** and milk
- **Whole Grain Pancakes** topped with fruit, served with canadian bacon, and milk
- Ramen noodles with choices of toppings such as grated cheese, chopped tomato, sliced hard boiled eggs, and chopped onion
- Stir fry vegetables with tofu or meat, serve with brown rice for extra nutrition
- **Omelets,** whole grain toast, fruit juice or milk
- Soft flour tortillas with refried beans and cheese, **Food Processor Frozen Yogurt** for dessert
- Home made or canned chili topped with corn chips and grated cheese, fresh fruit for dessert
- Crock pot meals that you can prepare in the morning
- Pasta, rice, canned or frozen vegetables and fruit, canned chicken, and tuna can be kept on hand for quick meals.

Chapter 5

Snacks

Healthy homemade snack foods for nibblers

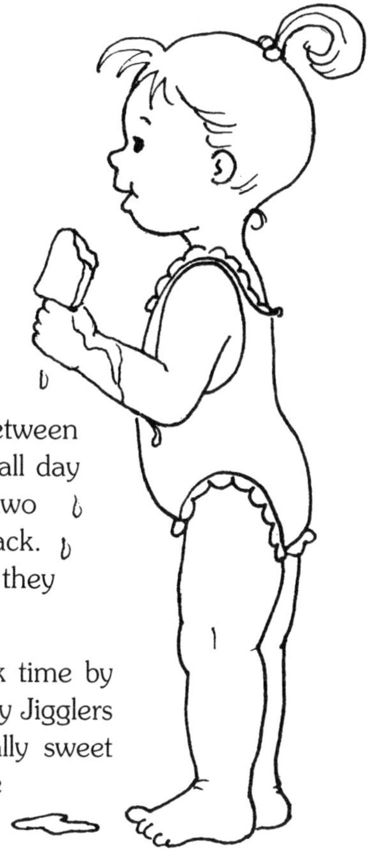

Preschoolers have small stomachs and need to eat between meals. Planning regular snack times helps prevent all day grazing or eating too close to mealtime. About two hours before the next meal is an ideal time for a snack. Preschoolers who still nap are usually hungry when they wake from an afternoon nap.

Encourage your child to eat vegetables at snack time by offering them with Dilly Dip. Fruit Leathers and Fruity Jigglers can be made ahead and kept on hand for naturally sweet treats. In the summer load the freezer with some frozen treats such as Banana Pops or Frozen Yogurt Sandwiches to keep young snackers cool on hot days.

Snack Recipes

1. *Yogurt Cheese*
2. *Pineapple Slush*
3. *Frozen Yogurt Sandwiches*
4. *Striped Fudgesicles*
5. *Banana Pops*
6. *Applesauce Gel Squares*
7. *Fruity Jigglers*
8. *Fruit Leather*
9. *Peanut Butter Dip*
10. *Fruit Dip*
11. *Dilly Dip*

Yogurt Cheese

A soft cheese that is fun to make and is similar to cream cheese.

3–4 sheets of cheesecloth

1 container (6–8 ounces) yogurt (lowfat doesn't work)

1. Line a colander or strainer with the sheets of cheesecloth and put it over a small bowl.
2. Pour off any extra liquid from yogurt. Stir yogurt and then spoon it onto the cheesecloth.
3. Gather together the edges of the cheesecloth and twist to form a bag of yogurt. Secure the top of the bag with a twist tie.
4. Leave the cheesecloth bag in the colander to allow liquid to continue to drain.
5. Refrigerate for at least 6 hours or overnight. Plain yogurt cheese will have the consistency of cream cheese. Fruit-flavored yogurt cheese will be softer.
6. Pour off and discard liquid before serving.

Serving suggestions:

Flavor plain yogurt cheese with sugar, honey or herbs if desired and use as a spread. Fruit-flavored yogurt cheese is good as a dip for fruit.

Yield: 1/3–1/2 cup

cook's tip:

Cotton cheesecloth is available at most supermarkets, hardware stores, and kitchen supply stores. Make sure it's marked for culinary use.

Pineapple Slush

This slushy drink is the perfect treat on a hot summer day! It is easy to make and kids love it.

1/2 cup frozen 100% pineapple juice concentrate (1/3 of a 12 ounce container)

2 cups crushed ice or 12 ice cubes

1/4 cup water

1. Put frozen juice concentrate in a blender with about a third of the ice.
2. Add a little of the water and slowly add the rest of the ice and water while blending.
3. Add additional water if the blender will not turn. Blend until smooth.

Serving suggestions:

Serve in bowls with a spoon or in a cup with a straw.

Yield: 2 cups

variations:

Any flavor frozen juice concentrate may be used in place of pineapple.

cook's tip:

Stop the blender occasionally and stir the mixture to speed up the blending time.

Frozen Yogurt Sandwiches

A great way to eat yogurt without a spoon. The graham crackers soften making them easy to eat.

8 whole graham crackers

1 container (8 ounces) yogurt, any flavor

1. Break graham crackers in half to make 16 square graham crackers.
2. Place 2 spoonfuls of yogurt on 8 of the graham cracker squares.
3. Top with the remaining crackers to make sandwiches.
4. Wrap individually in plastic wrap. Do not stack them or yogurt will seep out.
5. Freeze for at least 1 hour. May be kept in the freezer for up to 1 month.

Yield: 8 sandwiches

variations:

A 6 ounce container of yogurt will make 6 graham cracker sandwiches.

cook's tip:

Run hot water on outside of popsicle mold or cup to remove frozen fudgesicle.

variations:

Substitute peach yogurt for strawberry to make Tiger Pops.

Striped Fudgesicles

Frozen pudding and yogurt pops that pack a calcium punch.

1 cup chocolate pudding (1/2 small box, made according to directions)

1 container (6–8 ounces) strawberry yogurt

- ***popsicle molds or small paper cups***

1. Spoon a layer of pudding into popsicle molds or cups. Add a layer of yogurt.
2. Alternate layers of pudding and yogurt until within 1/4 inch of the top of container.
3. Put lids on popsicle molds or place plastic wrap over cups. Make a slit in the middle of wrap and insert a popsicle stick in each cup.
4. Freeze until solid.

Yield: varies with size of popsicle mold or cup

Banana Pops

Bananas, peanut butter, and chocolate—
a sweet summer treat!

2 bananas

4 popsicle sticks

1/2 cup milk chocolate or semi-sweet chocolate chips

2 tablespoons creamy peanut butter

1. Line a cookie sheet or pie plate with waxed paper.
2. Cut bananas in half crosswise.
3. Peel bananas and put a popsicle stick in cut end of each half.
4. Put chocolate chips or milk chocolate into a small microwavable bowl.
5. Microwave for 45 seconds, then stir and cook for 20 second intervals, stirring after each interval until chocolate is melted.
6. Stir peanut butter into chocolate until well blended.
7. Dip bananas in sauce using a spoon to spread sauce over all of the banana.
8. Place bananas on waxed paper.
9. Freeze for 1 1/2 hours or more.

Yield: 4 pops

tot quote:

"This cook book is going to be so big it will be as big as the house because it has so many things."

cook's tip:

Unflavored gelatin can be found near the flavored gelatins (Jello for example) at a grocery store. It is great to have on hand for making finger gels from juice. One envelope (7 grams) gels one cup of liquid.

Applesauce Gel Squares

This healthy, sugar-free finger gelatin is a good transitional food for older babies who are ready for finger foods.

1 cup unsweetened applesauce
1/8 teaspoon cinnamon (optional)
2 cups cold apple juice
3 packages unflavored gelatin

1. In a small bowl mix applesauce and cinnamon and set aside.
2. Pour 1 cup cold apple juice into 8x8 inch pan and sprinkle gelatin on top.
3. Heat remaining 1 cup of apple juice in the microwave for 3 minutes or on the stovetop until boiling.
4. Stir boiling juice into gelatin and cold juice. Continue mixing until gelatin dissolves.
5. Stir in applesauce.
6. Refrigerate for 1/2 hour and then stir to keep applesauce evenly distributed. If you omit this step the applesauce settles to the bottom, but it still tastes great!
7. Refrigerate for an additional 2 1/2 hours or until firm.

Serving suggestions:

Cut into squares with a knife, or cut into shapes with cookie cutters.

Yield: 8x8 inch pan

Fruity Jigglers

Filled with natural fruit flavor, there is nothing artificial about these!

1 can (12 ounces) any flavor frozen 100% juice concentrate, thawed

3 envelopes unflavored gelatin

1 1/2 cups boiling water

1. Into a medium bowl pour juice concentrate and sprinkle gelatin on top. Let sit until gelatin softens (about 3 minutes).
2. Stir boiling water into juice and gelatin. Continue mixing until gelatin is completely dissolved.
3. Pour into minimuffin cups. (An 8x8 inch pan can also be used.)
4. Refrigerate for 3 hours or until firm.

Yield: 48 minijigglers

variations:

Put a small slice of banana, strawberry, or any soft fresh or canned fruit in each muffin cup before pouring in gelatin.

variations:

Baby food pears, apricots, plums, prunes, bananas, or sweet potatoes work well for single flavor leathers. Carrots and applesauce don't.

tot quote:

"This is good, let's make more."

Fruit Leather

Save money by making your own fruit leather. No artificial coloring or added sugar needed.Great to take on a hike or a camping trip.

1 large jar (6 ounces) banana-pineapple baby food

1 medium jar (4 ounces) prunes w/ apple baby food

OR:

1 large jar (6 ounces) sweet potato baby food

1 large jar (6 ounces) applesauce baby food

1/4 teaspoon cinnamon

1. Set oven to the lowest setting (150–200°).
2. Line a cookie sheet with plastic wrap.
3. Pour about 4 tablespoons of strained food mixture onto the wrap. Spread as evenly as possible with a spatula to make a 5x6 inch rectangle about 1/8 inch thick. (Use more mix to make larger leathers if desired.)
4. Repeat to use all of the mix, leaving an inch between leathers.
5. Put the cookie sheet into the oven and leave it for about 8–10 hours. The drying time will vary with the size of the leathers, the number of cookie sheets, and the temperature of your oven.
6. The leather is done when it is no longer sticky to the touch but is still flexible.
7. Cut through plastic wrap to separate leathers. Roll the plastic wrap and leather into a roll. Cut into shorter rolls with kitchen shears if desired.

Yield: 5–6 leathers

Peanut Butter Dip

Serve as a dip for celery sticks and slices of apple or pear.

1/2 cup creamy peanut butter
1/2 cup plain yogurt
1/2 teaspoon cinnamon

1. Place all ingredients into a small mixing bowl.
2. Stir until fluffy.

Yield: 1 cup

cook's tip:

This will keep for one week in a sealed container in the refrigerator.

tot quote:

"I like to dip the pretzels in it."

Fruit Dip

So creamy tasting you won't believe it's lowfat.

1/2 cup lowfat cream cheese
1/2 cup plain nonfat yogurt
2 tablespoons brown sugar
1 teaspoon vanilla

1. Place all ingredients into a small mixing bowl.
2. Stir until fluffy.

Serving suggestions:

Use as a dip for slices of apple or other fruits, vegetables, or pretzels.

Yield: 1 cup

Dilly Dip

Kids cannot get enough of this. They love to dip carrots and celery in it. Nonfat mayonnaise and sour cream may be used.

1/2 cup mayonnaise

1/2 cup sour cream

1 tablespoon dill weed

1/2 teaspoon Bon Appétit (or 1/4 teaspoon parsley flakes & 1/8 teaspoon salt)

1. Place all ingredients into a small bowl
2. Stir until well blended.

Serving suggestions:

Use as a dip for vegetables such as carrots, celery, zucchini, or green peppers. For children under three who may choke on raw vegetables, steam the vegetables lightly before serving.

Yield: 1 cup

tot tip:

Put a spoonful of mayonnaise and sour cream on the child's plate. Sprinkle dill weed and Bon Appétit on top and let them mix it themselves with a carrot or celery stick.

tot quote:

"I love it 1 billion. Cause I just love it because I love carrots."

Other Snack Ideas

- Banana slices, chunks of melon, or other fresh fruits, plain or dipped in yogurt
- Cubes of cheese and apple slices
- String cheese
- **Soft Pretzels** to dip in hummus or other healthy dips
- **Oatmeal Cookies** with milk
- Graham crackers or vanilla wafers to dip in milk
- Yogurt
- **Poached Pears**
- Cottage cheese plain or with fruit
- Bagel spread with cream cheese
- 100% fruit juice and **Vegetable Crackers**
- Vegetable juice
- Fruit smoothies (see **Beverage** Chapter)
- **Graham Cracker Applesauce Cake**
- Whole grain cereal and milk
- Muffins with milk (see **Breakfast** Chapter)
- Dry cereal, pretzels, and small crackers combined to make a homemade trail mix

Chapter 6

Desserts

Sweet treats for little sweethearts

Who doesn't love desserts? Satisfy your child's sweet tooth, and your own, with healthy desserts such as Easy Frozen Yogurt, High Fiber Cookies, or Poached Pears. These delicious desserts are nutritious enough to serve every night.

If your child generally eats a healthy variety of food an occasional treat is not a problem. Peanut butter fans will enjoy the yummy Peanut Butter Chocolate Chip Cookies or Peanut Butter Bars.

Dessert Recipes

1. Fruit Salad
2. Poached Pears
3. Easy Frozen Yogurt
4. Fruit Cocktail Cake
5. Banana Cookies
6. Oatmeal Cookies
7. High Fiber Cookies
8. Peanut Butter Chocolate Chip Cookies
9. Baby's First Cookie
10. Banana Cupcakes
11. Banana Frosting
12. Peanut Butter Bars
13. Peanut Butter Frosting

Fruit Salad

A nutritious and tasty ending to any meal.

1 can (15 ounces) fruit cocktail, undrained

1 can (15 ounces) diced peaches, undrained

1 small box instant pudding mix, cheesecake flavor is good

1 banana, sliced

1 apple, chopped

1. Into a medium bowl drain fruit cocktail and peach juice.
2. Add the pudding mix and beat until mixture thickens.
3. Mix fruit cocktail, peaches, banana, and apple into pudding.

Yield: 5 1/2 cups

variations:

Omit the pudding mix if you prefer. Fresh or frozen berries are a nice addition.

cook's tip:

Refrigerate leftover salad until morning. Puree it in blender with yogurt, milk, or juice to make a smoothie. Even if the fruit is slightly brown it will taste fine.

cook's tip:

Comice, red Bartlett, or Bosc pears work best.

Poached Pears

You won't believe that pears are the only ingredient in this creamy dessert. You can even mash up a little for baby.

2–4 ripe pears

1. Set oven to 350°.
2. Thoroughly wash each pear.
3. Prick each pear 3–4 times with a fork.
4. Place pears in an 8x8 inch pan with stems up.
5. Bake for 30–40 minutes or until the skin turns brown and juice starts dripping off pear. If you stick a fork in pears they should be soft.
6. Slice pears in half lengthwise.
7. Scoop stem thread and seeds out.
8. Place each 1/2 pear into a small bowl and eat by scooping out fruit with a spoon. (Do not eat peel.)

Serving suggestions:

Sprinkle with granola and top with a dab of whipped topping or cream.

Yield: 4–8 pear halves

Easy Frozen Yogurt

What a fun way to eat fruit! A healthy alternative to ice cream.

2 cups frozen whole strawberries
1/3 cup plain yogurt
3 tablespoons powdered sugar

1. Assemble food processor with metal blade.
2. Put strawberries, yogurt, and powdered sugar into the processor bowl.
3. Process until smooth, stopping as needed and stirring with spoon to evenly distribute fruit.
4. Serve immediately.

Yield: 1 1/2 cups

variations:

Frozen raspberries, sweet cherries, peaches, or blueberries. Add 1/2 banana for milder flavor.

cook's tip:

To freeze berries, put one layer washed fruit on a cookie sheet lined with waxed paper. Freeze until solid then put fruit in resealable freezer bags for longer storage.

Fruit Cocktail Cake

Quick and easy, this moist cake is delicious enough to serve to guests.

1 egg

1 small can (15 ounces) lightly sweetened fruit cocktail, undrained

1/2 cup sugar

1 cup flour

1 teaspoon baking soda

1 tablespoon brown sugar

1. Set oven to 325°.
2. Lightly grease 9 inch round cake pan.
3. In a medium bowl, beat egg lightly with a fork.
4. Stir in fruit cocktail and then sugar.
5. Sift flour and baking soda into fruit cocktail mixture and stir until well mixed.
6. Pour mixture into cake pan.
7. Lightly sprinkle the top with brown sugar.
8. Bake for 40–45 minutes or until toothpick inserted in center comes out clean.

Serving suggestions:

Good with whipped cream or whipped topping.

Yield: 9 inch round pan

Banana Cookies

Soft, cake-like cookies that are easy for young eaters to munch.

2/3 cup mashed ripe bananas (1 1/2–2 bananas)
2/3 cup shortening
1/2 cup sugar
2 eggs
1/3 cup milk
1 teaspoon vanilla
2 1/4 cups flour
2 teaspoons baking powder
1/4 teaspoon baking soda
1/4 teaspoon salt

1. Set oven to 350°.
2. Lightly spray a cookie sheet with vegetable oil cooking spray.
3. In a medium bowl blend bananas, shortening, sugar, eggs, milk, and vanilla.
4. Sift together flour, baking powder, baking soda, and salt.
5. Add flour mixture to banana mixture until combined.
6. Drop by spoonfuls unto cookie sheet.
7. Bake for 8–10 minutes or until set.

Yield: 3–4 dozen cookies

Tot quote:

"I always like to help my mom when she's making something like cookies."

variations:

Substitute 1/2 cup applesauce for 1/2 cup of the oil for a soft lower fat cookie.

tot quote:

"I like going to grandma's house because when I ask for a cookie, she never says no."

Oatmeal Cookies

A favorite family recipe, these cookies are perfect for dipping in milk.

2 eggs
1 cup vegetable oil
1/2 cup brown sugar
1/2 cup sugar
2 cups flour
2 teaspoons cinnamon
1 teaspoon nutmeg
1 teaspoon baking powder
1/4 teaspoon baking soda
2 cups oats
1 cup raisins

1. Set oven to 375°.
2. Lightly spray a cookie sheet with vegetable oil cooking spray.
3. In a mixing bowl beat eggs lightly.
4. Add oil and sugars and mix until fluffy.
5. Sift flour, cinnamon, nutmeg, baking powder, and baking soda into egg mixture and mix thoroughly.
6. Stir oats and raisins into dough.
7. Drop dough by spoonfuls or small scoop onto cookie sheet.
8. Bake for 10–12 minutes or until edges begin to brown.

Yield: 3–4 dozen cookies

High Fiber Cookies

Who would have thought that high fiber could be so yummy!

1/2 cup vegetable oil

1 egg

1/2 cup brown sugar

1 teaspoon vanilla

1 cup All Bran or similar cereal

1 cup quick cooking oats

1/2 cup flour

1/2 cup whole wheat flour

1/2 teaspoon baking soda

1/2 teaspoon baking powder

1/2 teaspoon salt

1/2 cup raisins

1. Set oven to 350°.
2. Lightly spray a cookie sheet with vegetable oil cooking spray.
3. In a mixing bowl beat together oil, egg, brown sugar, and vanilla until creamy.
4. Mix in bran cereal and oats.
5. Sift flours, baking soda, baking powder, and salt into egg mixture and mix well.
6. Stir in raisins.
7. Drop dough by spoonfuls or from a small scoop onto cookie sheet.
8. Bake for 8–10 minutes or until lightly browned.

Yield: 2 dozen cookies

cook's tip:

Consider using canola oil whenever vegetable oil is called for, it is more nutritious.

tot quote:

"I kind of don't know why I like cookies, I just do."

Peanut Butter Chocolate Chip Cookies

Everyone loves chocolate chip cookies. This is our favorite version of a classic.

1 cup smooth peanut butter
1 cup butter or margarine
1 cup sugar
1 cup brown sugar
2 eggs
2 1/2 cups flour
1 1/2 teaspoons baking soda
1 teaspoon baking powder
1 cup semi-sweet chocolate chips
1 cup peanut butter chips

1. In a mixing bowl blend peanut butter, butter, sugar, and brown sugar.
2. Add eggs to peanut butter mixture and mix until smooth.
3. Sift flour, baking soda, and baking powder and add slowly to peanut butter mixture.
4. Stir in chocolate chips and peanut butter chips.
5. Cover and refrigerate dough at least 1 hour to chill.
6. When ready to bake, preheat oven to 375°.
7. Roll dough into 1 inch balls and gently flatten them down onto ungreased cookie sheet.
8. Bake for 7–8 minutes or until edges begin to brown.
9. Remove from oven and cool for 1–2 minutes before removing from cookie sheet.

Yield: 4 dozen cookies

Baby's First Cookie

These nutritious cookies are soft and easy to eat, perfect for babies who can handle finger foods. Older children like them too!

1/2 cup butter or margarine

3/4 cup sugar

1 egg

1 large jar (6 ounces) baby food carrots

1 1/2 cups flour

1/4 cup powdered infant formula or powdered milk

1 1/2 teaspoons baking powder

1/2 teaspoon cinnamon

1 cup infant oat cereal

1. Set oven to 375°.
2. Lightly spray a cookie sheet with vegetable oil cooking spray.
3. In a medium bowl cream together butter and sugar. Mix in egg until smooth. Mix in baby food.
4. Sift flour, infant formula, baking powder, and cinnamon into egg mixture and stir until well blended.
5. Stir cereal into flour mixture.
6. Drop by spoonfuls onto cookie sheet.
7. Bake for 12 minutes or until edges are lightly browned.

Yield: 4 dozen cookies

variations:

Substitute baby food plums for a milder flavor.

tot quote:

"I like them because they have good things in them."

Banana Cupcakes

These nutritious cupcakes can be served plain or dressed up with Banana Frosting.

2 3/4 cups flour
2 teaspoons baking powder
1 1/2 teaspoons cinnamon
1 teaspoon baking soda
3/4 teaspoon nutmeg
1/2 teaspoon salt
1/4 teaspoon ground cloves
3/4 cup sugar
1/2 cup vegetable oil
2 eggs
1 2/3 cups mashed ripe bananas (4–5 bananas)
1/2 cup milk
2 teaspoons vanilla

1. Set oven to 350°
2. Lightly grease muffin pan or use paper liners.
3. Sift flour, baking powder, cinnamon, baking soda, nutmeg, salt, and cloves together.
4. In a large bowl beat sugar, oil, and eggs until fluffy.
5. Add flour mixture and bananas alternately to sugar mixture, beating well after each addition.
6. Stir milk and vanilla into mixture.
7. Fill muffin cups 2/3 full.
8. Bake 17–19 minutes for regular cupcakes, 10–12 minutes for minicupcakes or until tops spring back when lightly touched.

Yield: 18 medium cupcakes or 48 minicupcakes

Banana Frosting

Delicious on cakes or cupcakes.

1/4 cup mashed ripe banana–about 1/2 of a medium banana

3 tablespoons butter or margarine

1 teaspoon vanilla

2 cups powdered sugar

1. In an electric mixer bowl blend banana, butter, and vanilla.
2. Gradually sift powdered sugar into banana mixture while continuing to mix. Slightly more or less sugar can be used to make frosting the desired consistency.

Yield: 1 cup, frosts an 8x8 inch cake or 18 cupcakes

tot quote:

"It's like I never want them to be gone."

Peanut Butter Bars

If your family loves peanut butter these are sure to be a hit!

2/3 cup creamy peanut butter
3/4 cup brown sugar
2 eggs
1 teaspoon vanilla
3/4 cup flour
1/2 teaspoon baking powder

1. Set oven to 350°.
2. Lightly grease an 8x8 inch baking pan.
3. In a mixing bowl beat together peanut butter, brown sugar, eggs, and vanilla until smooth.
4. Sift in flour and baking powder and mix well.
5. Spoon batter into baking pan.
6. Bake for 21–24 minutes or until toothpick inserted into the middle comes out clean.

Serving suggestions:

Spread with Peanut Butter Frosting if desired and cut into squares.

Yield: 8x8 inch pan

Peanut Butter Frosting

A creamy, flavorful frosting.

1/4 cup creamy peanut butter
1 1/4 cups powdered sugar, sifted
2 tablespoons milk
1 teaspoon vanilla

1. Place peanut butter in a mixing bowl.
2. Alternately add powdered sugar and milk, beating well after each addition.
3. Add vanilla to peanut butter mixture and mix well.
4. Add more milk or powdered sugar if needed for a good spreading consistency.
5. Spread on cake or bar cookies.

Yield: 3/4 cup, frosts an 8x8 inch cake

cook's tip:

This makes a great frosting for a chocolate cake.

Other Dessert Ideas

- Muffins containing fruit or spread with jam (see **Breakfast** Chapter)
- Fresh, frozen, or canned fruit
- Graham crackers or vanilla wafers to dunk in a cup of chocolate milk
- Ice cream topped with berries, sliced bananas, or other fresh or frozen fruits
- Fruit smoothies (see **Breakfast** chapter)
- Homemade or boxed puddings made with milk
- Layer yogurt, fresh or frozen fruit, and **Muesli**
- Fresh fruit with **Fruit Dip**
- Toasted frozen waffle square with berries and a dab of whipped topping or cream
- **Chocolate Dipped Fruit**
- **Fruity Jigglers**
- **Crepes** filled with fruit or jam, topped with whipped topping or cream
- Fruit-flavored yogurt
- Baked apples

Chapter 7

Little Helpers

Hands-on experience for budding chefs

Many good cooks have wonderful childhood memories of helping their parents or grandparents in the kitchen. Children love to be involved with food preparation. Even the most active little ones can stay enthusiastically engaged in a cooking project. Cooking is a great science experiment. Ingredients are combined to make something new. Baking significantly changes the appearance of the original mixture—almost like magic!

Involving a preschooler with food preparation is a good way to overcome objections to new foods. A child who helps cook the food may be more willing to try it. Helping in the kitchen can also be a sensory activity. It involves feeling, tasting, and smelling. Try our No-Bake Cookies for example.

You may be surprised how much your little one enjoys participating in a cooking project. What's more, when your child is a teenager, you might have a willing kitchen helper!

Little Helpers Recipes

1. *Vegetable Crackers*
2. *Cheezy Pretzels*
3. *Butter*
4. *Graham Cracker Applesauce Cake*
5. *Easy Banana Cream Dessert*
6. *Fruit Mini Pies*
7. *No-Bake Cookies*
8. *Sour Cream Sugar Cookies*
9. *Fruit Pizza*
10. *Ice Cube Tray Popsicles*
11. *Ten-Day Squish Bread*
12. *Krazy Kake*
13. *Pudding Frosting*

Vegetable Crackers

Fun to make and healthy too! Toddlers will love discovering how to create their own crackers.

1 1/2 cups quick cooking oats

1 cup flour

1/2 cup wheat germ

1 1/2 tablespoons sugar

1/2 teaspoon salt

1 jar (4 ounces) mixed vegetable baby food

1/3 cup vegetable oil

1 tablespoon water

1. Set oven to 350°.
2. Lightly spray a cookie sheet with vegetable oil spray.
3. In a medium bowl combine oats, flour, wheat germ, sugar, and salt.
4. Mix baby food, oil, and water into oatmeal mixture.
5. Roll out onto a cookie sheet to 1/16–1/8 of an inch.
6. Sprinkle with salt and lightly roll again to press salt in.
7. Cut into squares or diamonds with a pizza cutter or knife. (You can also use small cookie cutters.)
8. Place cookie sheet in oven and check after 25 minutes. The outer crackers will cook first. Remove crackers as they turn light brown and hard.

Yield: 16 dozen 1 inch square crackers, equivalent to a small box of crackers

variations:

Use 1/2 cup water instead of the strained vegetables & water

tot tip:

Cook less time for a softer cracker that is perfect for the young toddler.

Cheezy Pretzels

These pretzels turn out soft and moist, just perfect for toddlers. Kids can form them into the traditional shape or make letters, numbers, or snakes and then sprinkle on the toppings.

1 1/2 cups warm water

1 tablespoon dry yeast

1 tablespoon sugar

4 cups flour

1/2 cup instant powdered milk

1/2 teaspoon salt

1 cup grated mozzarella cheese (about 1/4 pound)

1 beaten egg

Topping Options:

- ***sesame seeds***
- ***grated parmesan cheese***
- ***salt***

1. Set oven to 425°.
2. Lightly spray a cookie sheet with vegetable oil spray.
3. Put warm water into measuring cup and sprinkle yeast and sugar onto water.
4. In a large bowl combine 3 cups of the flour, the powdered milk, and salt.
5. Slowly add yeast mixture to flour mixture and stir until well mixed.
6. Add last cup of flour and the mozzarella cheese.

7. Knead for several minutes on a floured surface.
8. Make 16 inch ropes (snakes) and then shape them into pretzels or let kids make any shapes they want.
9. Arrange pretzels on cookie sheet.
10. Brush pretzel with egg and then sprinkle with toppings.
11. Bake for 11–13 minutes or until just starting to brown.

Yield: 24 medium pretzels

tot tip:

Little helpers can practice measuring and pouring while making these.

Butter

Preschoolers will learn how butter is made with this easy recipe. Try dipping pretzels in it.

1/4 cup heavy cream at room temperature

1 clean empty baby food jar with lid (6 ounce size)

4 inch square piece of tin foil (optional)

1/16 teaspoon salt

1. Pour cream into baby food jar.
2. Make a ball from the tin foil and place in jar. This will help stir cream and will speed up the process.
3. Screw lid on tightly.
4. Shake jar. Cream will first look whipped, keep shaking until it separates into buttermilk and soft butter (like whipped butter).
5. Drain off buttermilk and remove tin foil ball. Stir in salt.

Serving suggestions:

Try with bread or our favorite, Cheezy Pretzels.

Yield: about 3 tablespoons

Graham Cracker Applesauce Dessert

A simply delicious, easy to make layered cake. Older preschoolers can do this one by themselves.

15 whole cinnamon graham crackers (30 squares)

2 cups applesauce

1. Cover the bottom of an 8x8 inch pan with one layer of graham crackers, breaking crackers as needed. (3–4 whole crackers)
2. Spread 2/3 cup of the applesauce over graham crackers.
3. Repeat with two more layers of graham crackers and applesauce.
4. Top with a layer of graham crackers.
5. Refrigerate for at least 30 minutes or until crackers are soft.

Serving suggestions:

Serve plain or with a spoonful of whipped topping.

Yield: 8x8 inch pan

Tot quotes:

"I bet this is the best cake ever."

"This is the best dessert. I love it better than Cheetos. More than you think."

variations:

Try other flavors of pudding, chocolate graham crackers.

Easy Banana Cream Dessert

This dessert is similar to banana cream pie, but much faster because there is no pie crust to make. Little helpers can squish the pudding, break and arrange the graham crackers, cut bananas with a plastic knife, and sprinkle on the crumbs.

1 small box instant vanilla pudding mix

2 cups milk, 2% or whole milk works best

1 resealable freezer bag, gallon size

2 cups frozen whipped topping, thawed or 1 package prepared nondairy whipped topping

8 whole graham crackers (16 squares)

3 bananas

1 tablespoon graham cracker crumbs (1 cracker square)

1 tablespoon wheat germ (optional)

1. Put pudding mix and milk into plastic bag. Be sure bag is well sealed.
2. Squeeze and shake the bag until pudding is thoroughly mixed and thickened.
3. Add 1 cup of whipped topping to the pudding in the bag and reseal it. Squeeze the bag until the topping and pudding are well mixed.
4. Cover the bottom of an 8x8 inch pan with one layer of graham crackers, breaking crackers as needed.
5. Add layer of sliced bananas.
6. Cut diagonally across one corner of the bag and

squeeze half of the pudding out onto the layer of bananas. Spread evenly over bananas.

7. Repeat with additional layers of graham crackers, bananas, and the second half of the pudding.
8. Top with remaining whipped topping.
9. Mix cracker crumbs and wheat germ and sprinkle on top.
10. Refrigerate for about 2 hours to soften crackers and chill dessert, then cut into squares and serve.

Yield: 8x8 inch pan, double the recipe for a 9x13 inch pan

cook's tip:

Put 1 graham cracker square into a resealable plastic bag and roll it with a rolling pin to make crumbs.

cook's tip:

To make cinnamon-sugar combine 1 tablespoon sugar & 1 teaspoon cinnamon.

Fruit Mini Pies

Fun and easy to make. These can also be made with bread or roll dough.

1 package (7 1/2 ounces) refrigerator biscuits
1 small apple, peeled & chopped
- ***cinnamon sugar***

1. Set oven to 400°.
2. Lightly grease a minimuffin pan.
3. Flatten out each biscuit by pressing and stretching gently.
4. Place each flattened biscuit in a minimuffin cup.
5. Put 1 heaping teaspoon chopped apple into biscuit, sprinkle with cinnamon sugar, and pinch together the top edges of the biscuit.
6. Spray pies lightly with non-stick oil spray and sprinkle with more cinnamon sugar.
7. Put a little water into any empty muffin cups.
8. Bake for 8–10 minutes or until lightly browned.

Yield: 10 mini pies

No-Bake Cookies

A cookie that is so easy, kids can do most of the work. Just make sure the chocolate is cooled before little ones help.

1/2 cup chocolate chips

1/3 cup powdered milk

1/3 cup creamy peanut butter

1/4 cup graham cracker crumbs (1 1/2 crackers)

2/3 cup oats

Coating:

3 tablespoons graham cracker crumbs (1 whole cracker)

1. Pour chocolate chips into medium sized glass bowl.
2. Microwave for 45 seconds, then stir and cook for 20 second intervals, stirring each time until chocolate is melted.
3. Stir in powdered milk.
4. Add peanut butter and stir until combined.
5. Stir in graham cracker crumbs and oats. Add a little more oats, if needed, to make a stiff dough.
6. Form into 1 inch balls and roll in graham cracker crumbs to coat.

Yield: 1 1/2 dozen cookies

tot quote:

"I like to mix it. That is my favorite part."

cook's tip:

Liquid egg substitute can be found near the eggs in the grocery.

Sour Cream Sugar Cookies

Perfect for little mouths, these cookies are soft and light. The egg substitute makes the dough safe to sample.

1/2 cup butter or margarine
1 1/2 cups powdered sugar
1 teaspoon vanilla
1/4 cup egg substitute
1/2 teaspoon almond extract
1/2 cup light sour cream
3 cups flour
1 teaspoon baking soda
1 teaspoon cream of tartar

1. Set oven to 350°.
2. Cream butter, sugar, vanilla, egg substitute and almond extract.
3. Mix in sour cream.
4. Sift together flour, baking soda, and cream of tartar.
5. Stir flour mixture into butter mixture until blended.
6. On lightly floured surface roll out dough to 1/8 inch thickness. The cookies will rise during baking.
7. Use cookie cutters to cut into shapes. Choose decorating options.
8. Place on ungreased cookie sheet and bake for 7–9 minutes or until set.

Decorating options:

Before baking: Mix 1/2 tablespoon egg substitute and 5–7 drops food coloring and use clean watercolor brush to paint cookies. Or sprinkle with colored sugar made with 1 tablespoon sugar and 3 drops food coloring.

After baking: Frost or decorate with frosting and sprinkles as desired.

Yield: 4 dozen medium cookies

tot quote:

"My favorite part about making them is the dough eating."

variation:

Use fresh pineapple, blueberries, raspberries, nectarines, etc.

tot tip:

Make individual pizzas and let kids top their own with fruit.

Fruit Pizza

A delicious dessert pizza—looks as good as it tastes.

- ***Sour Cream Sugar Cookie dough or 18 ounce package sugar cookie refrigerator dough***

1 package (8 ounces) cream cheese, softened

1/4 cup powdered sugar

1 can (20 ounces) pineapple tidbits, drained, reserve 5 tablespoons juice

3–4 kiwi fruits peeled & thinly sliced

2 cups fresh strawberries, washed and sliced

1. Set oven to 350°.
2. Roll out sugar cookie dough onto 14–16 inch pizza pan (12 inch pan for refrigerator dough).
3. Bake for 12–15 minutes or until edges are just beginning to brown.
4. Whip cream cheese, sugar, and 5 tablespoons pineapple juice until creamy.
5. Spread cream cheese mixture onto cooled crust.
6. Arrange pineapple around outer edge of pizza, then a circle of kiwi fruit, then strawberries. Repeat until surface is covered.
7. Refrigerate until serving. Will keep for up to 24 hours, best if served immediately.

Yield: 12–16 inch pizza

Ice Cube Tray Popsicles

Preschoolers can perfect their pouring skills while making these healthy popsicles.

- ***juice***
- ***toothpicks***

1. Pour juice into ice cube tray.
2. Cover with plastic wrap and poke a toothpick into the middle of each square.
3. Put into freezer and freeze until solid.

tot quotes:

"My favorite part about making them is making the juice because I love to stir it."

"My favorite part is to eat them."

tot tip:

Supervise children while they eat these as toothpicks can be choking hazards.

variations:

Use chocolate, banana, lemon, white chocolate, or coconut pudding mix. Add 1 cup of nuts, raisins, blueberries, dried cranberries, or chocolate chips.

Ten-Day Squish Bread

Toddlers will love to squish the bag each day. They can practice sharing by giving friends starter for this sweet bread.

Sourdough starter:

1/3 cup whole wheat flour

1/3 cup plain yogurt

1/3 cup sugar

Day One

1. Place flour, yogurt, and sugar into a gallon-sized resealable freezer bag.
2. Seal the bag and squish it until contents are well mixed.
3. Put bag into a bowl and leave at room temperature.

Day Two, Three, Four, and Five

Squish the bag each day.

Day Six

1 cup white flour

1 cup sugar

1 cup yogurt

1. Add flour, sugar, and yogurt and then squish the bag to mix. Leave at room temperature.

Day Seven, Eight, and Nine

1. Squish the bag each day.

Day Ten

1 cup white flour

1 cup sugar

1 cup milk

1. Pour the bag of starter into a large nonmetallic mixing bowl.
2. Stir in flour, sugar, and milk.
3. Pour 1 cup of mixture into each of four resealable one quart bags. Keep one for yourself and give the other three to friends with a copy of the recipe. Keep starter in the refrigerator until you're ready to make a new batch.
4. To the remaining batter in the bowl add:

1 cup vegetable oil

3 eggs

1/2 cup milk

1 teaspoon vanilla

2 cups white flour

1 large box instant vanilla pudding mix

1 cup sugar

2 teaspoons cinnamon

1 1/2 teaspoons baking powder

1/2 teaspoon baking soda

1/4 teaspoon salt

1. Set oven to 350°.
2. Grease two loaf pans and dust with a mix of cinnamon and sugar if desired.
3. Pour batter into pans and bake for 1 hour and 15 minutes or until a toothpick inserted in center of loaf comes out clean.

Yield: 2 loaves, 3 sourdough starters

tot quote:

"We have to go squish the bread!"

tot tip:

No eggs means little helpers can sample the batter.

Krazy Kake

No bowls to wash! Kids can mix this cake right in the pan. All you have to do is pop it in the oven.

2 1/4 cups flour
1 1/2 cups sugar
4 1/2 tablespoons unsweetened cocoa powder
1 1/2 teaspoons baking soda
3/4 teaspoon salt
1/2 cup oil
1 1/2 teaspoons white vinegar
1 1/2 teaspoons vanilla
1 1/2 cups water

1. Set oven to 325°.
2. Into a 9x13 inch cake pan sift flour, sugar, cocoa, soda, and salt. Poke three holes in mixture.
3. Pour oil into one hole, vinegar into the 2nd, and vanilla into the 3rd.
4. Pour water over all and stir until blended.
5. Bake for 30 minutes or until top springs back when lightly touched.

Serving suggestions:

Frost with Pudding Frosting or Peanut Butter Frosting.

Yield: 9x13 inch pan

Pudding Frosting

Squish and squeeze to make this fun frosting. Good frosting for cakes or just spread on graham crackers for a treat.

1 small box instant pudding mix, any flavor

2 cups half & half

1 resealable freezer bag, quart size

1. Put pudding mix and half and half into the plastic bag. Be sure bag is well-sealed.
2. Squeeze and shake the bag until pudding is thoroughly mixed and thickened.
3. Cut diagonally across one bottom corner of the bag and squeeze pudding frosting onto cake.
4. Spread frosting evenly over cake.
5. Refrigerate cake until ready to serve and keep any leftovers in the refrigerator.

Yield: 2 cups

Other Little Helper Ideas

- Don't forget to have children wash their hands before helping with food preparation.
- Set out all the ingredients and equipment, such as measuring cups and spoons, before you start and the project will go more smoothly.
- Provide a step stool for your child to stand on to easily reach the counter top.
- Consider protecting your countertop, table, or other working surface with waxed paper. You can just gather it up, crumbs, spills and all and throw it away when you finish.
- Teach your child kitchen safety rules while you work together in the kitchen.
- Be careful about little fingers and electric mixers. Don't leave a child unattended with a mixer running.
- Use kitchen gadgets such as egg slicers and melon ball cutters to make food more fun.
- Don't let your child taste batters or doughs that contain raw eggs unless you use pasteurized eggs or egg substitutes.
- Help your tot develop beginning math skills while measuring ingredients for recipes.
- Consider activities young children can help with including: shucking corn and pulling the cornsilk off, tearing lettuce for salad, opening packages, stirring batters, kneading and shaping dough, spreading butter or other spreads on sandwiches.

Chapter 8

Special Times

Great ideas for holidays and birthdays

Whether it's Baby's first birthday, a preschooler's birthday party, or a holiday, make it more fun with special food. Try Sweetheart Cupcakes for an easy valentine treat or make our Ice Cream Cone Cakes to please a birthday crowd. Decorating a Gingerbread House is a great way to spend family time during the busy holidays. They'll look forward to it every year.

Special Times Recipes

Valentine's Day

1. *Chocolate Dipped Fruit*
2. *Sweetheart Cupcakes*
3. *Cream Cheese Frosting*

Easter

1. *Perfect Hardboiled Eggs*
2. *Colored Eggs*

Halloween

1. *Caramel Apple Dip*
2. *Pumpkin Packed Cookies*

Thanksgiving

1. *No-Bake Pumpkin Pie*

Christmas

1. *Eggnog Bread*
2. *Gingerbread House*
3. *Dough Ornaments*
4. *Cinnamon-Applesauce Ornaments*

Birthdays

1. *Baby's First Cake*
2. *Ice Cream Cone Cakes*
3. *Confetti Sticks*

Chocolate Dipped Fruit

Preschoolers will love making these as a surprise for someone special.

1/2 cup chocolate chips

1 teaspoon vegetable oil

- ***fresh or dried fruit for dipping***

1. Line a cookie sheet with wax paper.
2. Place chocolate chips in a small bowl.
3. Microwave for 45 seconds, then stir and cook for 20 second intervals, stirring after each interval until chocolate is melted.
4. Stir in oil.
5. Dip fruit in chocolate and place on wax paper.
6. Refrigerate for about 15 minutes or until chocolate has hardened.

Yield: 1/3 cup dipping sauce

cook's tip:

You can also dip sugar cookies, shortbread, or graham crackers in chocolate dip.

cook's tip:

You can also make a giant heart by baking cake in an 8x8 inch square pan and an 8 inch circle pan. Cut circle cake in half and place halves onto two adjacent sides of the square cake.

Sweetheart Cupcakes

These fun, easy-to-make cupcakes will please any sweethearts, big or small.

1 box cake mix, any variety

- ***other ingredients listed on box***

1. Set oven according to cake mix directions.
2. Line muffin cups with paper liners.
3. Prepare cake mix according to package directions.
4. Spoon batter into muffin cups, filling them 3/4 full.
5. Make small balls of tin foil and place one between each liner and cup to make a heart shape.
6. Bake according to cake mix directions.
7. Cool and frost with Cream Cheese Frosting.

Yield: 24 cupcakes

Cream Cheese Frosting

A great topping for Sweetheart Cupcakes. Leave out the red food coloring to frost other cakes.

4 ounces cream cheese, softened

2 cups powdered sugar, sifted

1 teaspoon vanilla

1 teaspoon milk

- ***red food coloring***
- ***sprinkles (optional)***

1. With an electric mixer beat cream cheese at medium speed.
2. Gradually add sugar, continuing to beat until mixture is fluffy.
3. Stir in vanilla.
4. Add red food coloring until frosting is pink.
5. Spread on cake or cupcakes and top with sprinkles if desired.

Yield: 1 cup, frosts an 8x8 inch cake or 18 cupcakes

cook's tip:

For an easy cookie, spread this frosting between graham crackers.

cook's tip:

Hard-boiled eggs should not be kept out of the refrigerator for more than two hours.

Perfect Hardboiled Eggs

You can make perfect hard-boiled eggs every time with these easy directions.

- ***eggs***
- ***salt***

1. Put eggs in a saucepan and add cold water to at least 1 inch above eggs.
2. Add a pinch of salt to the water. If any eggs crack, it will stop the egg from leaking out while cooking.
3. Bring water to a rolling boil over high heat. Remove pan from heat to prevent further cooking, cover the pan, and let it sit for 18 minutes. Cooking eggs for too long causes them to have tough whites and dark rings around the yolks.
4. Run cold water over the eggs until they are cooled.
5. Refrigerate until ready to use. They can be kept up to 1 week in the refrigerator.
6. To peel boiled eggs, crack the shell by tapping it on a hard surface, then roll egg between your hands to loosen the shell. Start to peel at the large end where the air pocket is located. Holding the egg under cold running water will help slip the shell off.

Colored Eggs

A simple way to decorate eggs with ingredients from your kitchen.

3/4 cup water
1 teaspoon white vinegar
- ***food coloring***

1. Put water and vinegar into bowls large enough to allow water to cover an egg. Use one container for each color.
2. Add drops of food coloring to water until desired color is reached.
3. Put one hard-boiled egg at a time into colored water. Tongs are handy for this.
4. Leave the egg as long as it takes to get the color you want.
5. Refrigerate eggs.

cook's tip:

Use only food coloring or commercial egg dye. Paints can seep through the shells and might be toxic.

tot tip:

Children can use crayons to write their name or draw a picture on the eggs before dipping them.

Caramel Apple Dip

A fast version of a traditional holiday food. Apples can be peeled and thinly sliced for young eaters.

8 square caramels

1/2 tablespoon milk

1 sliced apple (Granny Smith apples are good)

1. Unwrap caramels and place in a small glass bowl.
2. Microwave on high for 30 seconds.
3. Stir in milk.
4. Microwave for 10 second intervals, stirring after each interval, until caramels are all melted.

Serving suggestions:

Dip apple slices in caramel and eat!

Yield: 2 1/2 tablespoons dip

Pumpkin-Packed Cookies

These soft, cake-like cookies are a great treat for Halloween or any time of year.

1 1/2 cups canned pumpkin
2/3 cup shortening
1 cup sugar
2 eggs
1/3 cup milk
1/2 teaspoon vanilla
2 1/4 cups flour
1/4 teaspoon baking soda
2 teaspoons baking powder
1/2 teaspoon salt
1/2 teaspoon nutmeg
1 1/2 teaspoons cinnamon
1 cup chocolate chips or raisins (optional)

1. Set oven to 350°.
2. Lightly spray a cookie sheet with vegetable oil cooking spray.
3. Cream together pumpkin, shortening, sugar, eggs, milk, and vanilla.
4. Sift together flour, baking soda, baking powder, salt, nutmeg, and cinnamon.
5. Slowly add flour mixture to pumpkin mixture and mix until combined.
6. Stir in chocolate chips or raisins.
7. Drop by spoonfuls onto cookie sheet.
8. Bake 12–14 minutes or until cookies are set.

Yield: 3–4 dozen cookies

tot tip:

Instead of mixing the chocolate chips or raisins into the dough, let your toddler place them on the cookies to make pumpkin faces.

tot quote:

"I like to eat it"

No-Bake Pumpkin Pie

Save time and please your family. Young children usually prefer this delicious holiday pie as it has a milder flavor and lighter texture than traditional pumpkin pie.

2/3 cup milk (2% or whole works best)

1 envelope (1.3 ounce) dry whipped topping mix (such as Dream Whip)

1 small box instant vanilla pudding

1 cup canned pumpkin

1/2 teaspoon cinnamon

1/2 teaspoon nutmeg

1/4 teaspoon ginger

1 nine inch baked pie shell or purchased graham cracker pie crust

1. Pour milk into mixer bowl and sprinkle in topping mix and pudding mix.
2. Beat until thickened.
3. Add pumpkin, cinnamon, nutmeg, and ginger and beat until well mixed.
4. Pour into a baked shell or a prepared graham cracker crust and chill in refrigerator until ready to serve.

Serving suggestions:

Top with whipped topping or whipped cream.

Yield: 1 pie

For three pies: use 3 envelopes dry whipped topping mix, 2 cups of milk, 2 packages of instant vanilla pudding, 1 package of instant lemon pudding, 1 large can of pumpkin (29 ounces), 1 1/2 teaspoons cinnamon, 1 1/2 teaspoons nutmeg, 3/4 teaspoon ginger, and 3 pie shells.

Eggnog Bread

An easy-to-make holiday bread with a traditional flavor.

3/4 cup sugar
1/4 cup oil
2 eggs
2 cups sifted flour
1 tablespoon baking powder
1/2 teaspoon nutmeg
1/2 teaspoon cinnamon
1/2 teaspoon salt
1 cup eggnog

1. Set oven to 350°.
2. Lightly grease one loaf pan.
3. In a large bowl combine sugar, oil, and eggs and mix well.
4. Sift together flour, baking powder, nutmeg, cinnamon, and salt.
5. Stir flour mixture into egg mixture, alternating with egg nog.
6. Mix only until dry ingredients are moistened.
7. Spoon into pan and bake for 50 minutes or until a toothpick inserted in the center comes out clean.

Yield: 1 loaf

cook's tip:

Make sure that children do not drink homemade eggnog that contains unpasteurized eggs. There is a risk of salmonella poisoning.

tot tip:

Don't allow children under the age of four to eat hard candies due to choking hazard.

Gingerbread House

Make this a holiday tradition. Double the batch and invite another family to bring some candy for decorating.

3/4 cup molasses

1/2 cup vegetable oil

1/3 cup brown sugar

1 egg

3 1/2 cups flour

1 tablespoon baking powder

1 teaspoon salt

1 teaspoon cinnamon

1/2 teaspoon ginger

1/8 teaspoon ground cloves (optional)

Frosting glue

3 egg whites (reconstituted pasteurized dried egg whites)

3 1/2 cups powdered sugar, about 1 pound

1/2 teaspoon cream of tartar

Decoration Options:

- ***round cookies***
- ***teddy grahams***
- ***waffle cones for trees***
- ***gumdrops or other small candies***
- ***candy canes***
- ***pretzels for fences***
- ***marshmallows for snowmen***
- ***chocolate chips***

1. Using the drawing as a guide, make a paper pattern for the house.
2. Set oven to 300°.
3. Cover the back of a cookie sheet (13x17 inch or longer) with foil and generously grease the foil with shortening.
4. In a large mixing bowl, combine molasses, oil, brown sugar, and egg and mix thoroughly.
5. Sift dry ingredients and slowly add to molasses mixture. Mix until thoroughly blended.
6. With a floured rolling pin, roll out dough to fit the back of the cookie sheet. Dough should be about 1/3 inch thick.
7. Bake for 30–35 minutes or until edges start to harden.
8. Remove from oven and using the pattern, immediately cut into shapes with a sharp knife.
9. Let pieces cool and harden. They should be dry enough to hold their shapes, but not brittle. If the pieces seem too soft, return them to a 200° oven.

To make frosting:

1. Reconstitute egg whites per package directions. (Look for powdered pasteurized egg whites in the baking section of the grocery store.) Raw egg whites can be used but should not be eaten because of the salmonella risk.
2. Sift together powdered sugar and cream of tartar.
3. Beat egg whites while gradually adding powdered sugar mixture. Continue to beat until stiff peaks appear.
4. Keep bowl of frosting covered with a wet towel to prevent frosting from drying out until you use it.
5. Add food coloring to some of the frosting if desired.

tot quote:

"It's like I never want to be done doing this."

cook's tip:

Make the gingerbread and bake it the day before you plan to assemble the houses.

Assembling and decorating houses:

1. Cover a cookie sheet or piece of cardboard with tin foil to use as a base for the house.
2. Put some frosting into a pastry tube or a resealable plastic freezer bag. If using bag, cut off a corner to squeeze out frosting. Pipe frosting along edges of pieces as you assemble house. Use plenty of frosting and apply to all edges, inside, and outside seams. Hold pieces together for a few seconds then use cans of food to support sides while the frosting dries.
3. After the house is assembled use dabs of frosting to attach decorations. Stick two or three marshmallows together to make snowmen. Invert cones for trees and decorate with frosting and candies.

Yield: 1 gingerbread house

Gingerbread House pattern:

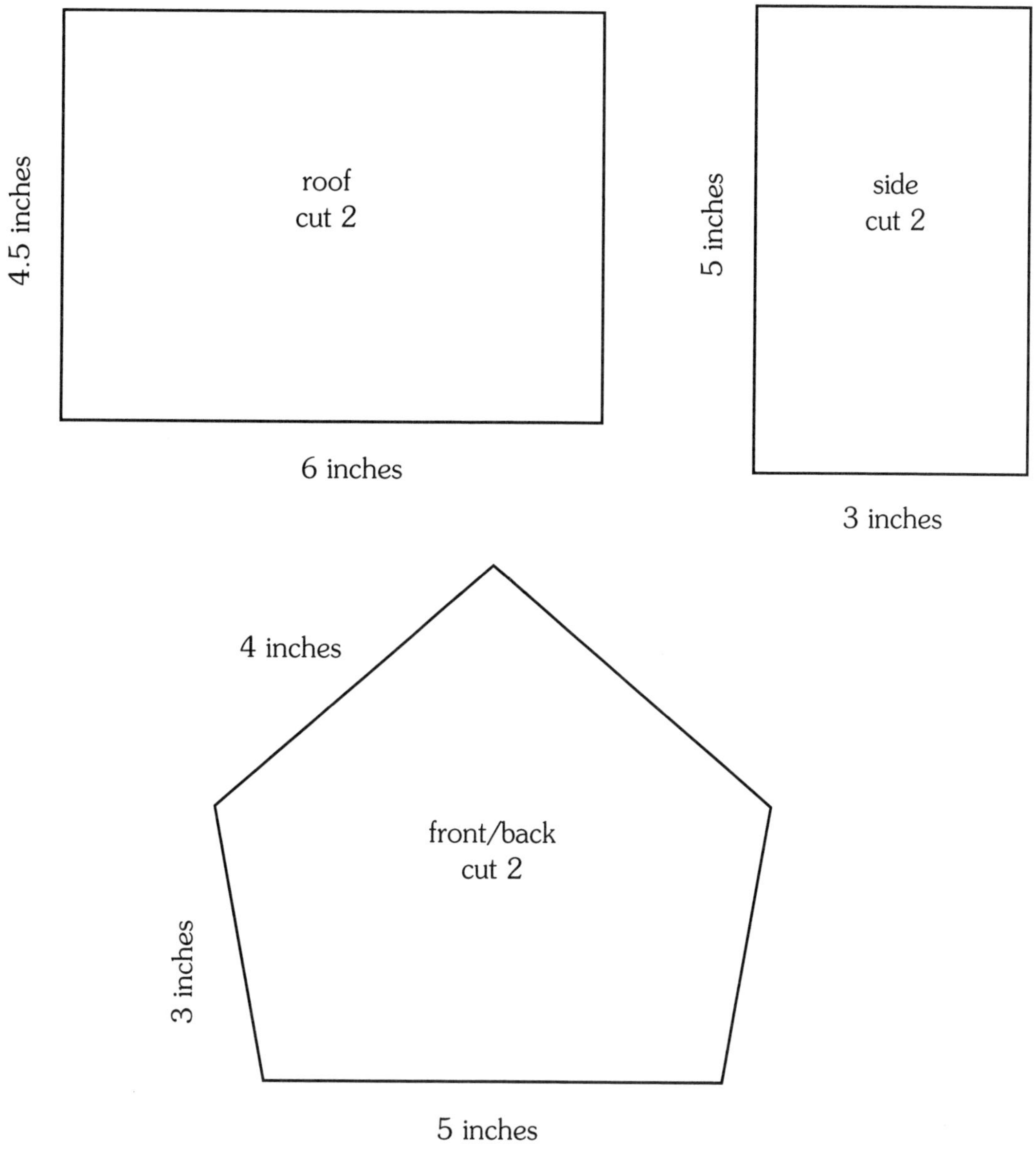

tot quote:

"It's certainly fun to get messy."

Dough Ornaments

These ornaments are great holiday gifts that children can give. When dry, they look like plaster and can be painted and decorated. The dough is also fun to play with, but does not keep long.

2 cups baking soda

1 cup cornstarch

1 1/4 cups cold water

- ***ribbon for hanging ornaments***

1. In a saucepan, combine baking soda and cornstarch.
2. Pour in cold water and cook over medium heat, stirring constantly for about 5 minutes, until mixture thickens.
3. Remove pan from heat and cover with a wet paper towel until cool.
4. When cool, knead on a waxed-paper covered surface until dough is smooth.
5. Roll out dough to about 1/6 inch thickness and cut with cookie cutters.
6. Make a hole in each ornament for ribbon.
7. Let air dry for 2 days, turning ornaments over periodically.
8. Paint ornaments or glue on sparkles.

Yield: 2–3 dozen ornaments

Cinnamon-Applesauce Ornaments

Let the kids decorate the tree this year. These simple ornaments will fill your house with a wonderful aroma.

1 cup applesauce

1 cup cinnamon

- ***ribbon for hanging ornaments***

1. Combine applesauce and cinnamon in a small bowl until it forms a dough. If dough is too wet add a little more cinnamon.
2. Roll out dough on wax paper to about 3/8 inch thickness.
3. Using small or medium sized cookie cutters, cut into Christmas shapes.
4. Place cut outs on a cookie sheet and make a hole in each for ribbon.
5. Let air dry 2–3 days. Periodically flip them over so both sides dry.
6. String with ribbon and hang on Christmas tree. They will be quite fragile after drying.

Yield: 12–15 medium ornaments

cook's tip:

To speed up the drying process, put in oven set to the lowest setting for 3–4 hours.

Baby's First Cake

A moist carrot cake without the bother of peeling and shredding the carrots.

2 jars (4 ounces each) carrot baby food
2 eggs
1/2 cup vegetable oil
1 cup sugar
1 teaspoon vanilla
1 cup flour
1 teaspoon cinnamon
1 teaspoon baking soda
1 teaspoon baking powder

1. Set oven to 350°.
2. Lightly grease an 8x8 inch baking pan.
3. With an electric mixer beat carrot baby food, sugar, eggs, oil, and vanilla.
4. Sift flour, cinnamon, soda, and baking powder into carrot mixture.
5. Continue to beat until thoroughly mixed.
6. Bake for 35–40 minutes.
7. Cool and serve or frost with Cream Cheese Frosting if desired.

Yield: 8x8 inch pan

variations:

Banana frosting is also good on this cake.

tot tip:

For baby's first birthday bake a small cake, frost with plenty of whipped cream, and let your little one dig in with both hands. Have your camera ready!

Ice Cream Cone Cakes

Eliminate the clean-up at an outdoor summer birthday party by putting a scoop of ice cream on each finished cone. You won't need plates or forks.

24 flat bottomed ice cream cones

1 box cake mix, any flavor

- ***other ingredients listed on box***

1. Set oven to 350°.
2. Make cake batter according to cake mix instructions.
3. Spoon batter into ice cream cones, filling them about 1/2 full.
4. Place cones on a cookie sheet
5. Bake for 20–25 minutes or until toothpick inserted in the center comes out clean.
5. Let cone cakes cool completely.

Serving suggestions:

Top each cone with a scoop of ice cream.

Yield: 24 cones

tot tip:

A good rule of thumb for children's birthday parties is to invite one guest for each year of age, unless you have adult help or are inviting entire families.

tot quote:

"Tasty!"

Confetti Sticks

A fun party treat that kids can make.

- ***decorating sprinkles***

1/2 cup white chocolate chips

1 teaspoon vegetable shortening

1 cup thin pretzel sticks

1. Line a cookie sheet with wax paper and put sprinkles in a small shallow bowl.
2. Place chocolate chips and shortening in a small bowl.
3. Microwave chocolate for 45 seconds, then stir and cook for 20 second intervals, stirring each time until chocolate is melted.
4. Dip pretzels halfway in chocolate until lightly coated.
5. Roll pretzel sticks in sprinkles and then lay on wax paper to cool.

Yield: 5–6 dozen small sticks

Birthday Party Ideas

- Have a *dress-up* birthday party. Invite the guests to wear dress-up clothes and to bring an item of dress-up clothing as a gift for the birthday child. Make **Rainbow Pasta** and let children make their own necklaces and bracelets as a party activity.
- Have a *teddy bear* picnic. Have guests bring their teddy bears (or other stuffed animals). Put a blanket on the floor in the winter or have the party outside in the summer and serve simple picnic foods. Give a box of animal crackers as a take home treat.
- Try a *vehicle* party theme. Suggest that guests bring gifts that go along with that theme. Give away matchbox cars or a car coloring book for party favors.
- For baby's first birthday throw a *rubber duck* party. Frost a round cake with light blue (or white) frosting and put several small rubber ducks on top. Blue and yellow balloons look great for decorations.
- Provide several colors of **Super Scented Play Dough,** rolling pins, garlic press, and cookie cutters and you'll keep preschoolers happy. Each party guest can take home a container of playdough as a party favor.
- Make **Fruity Jigglers** and cut them into shapes with cookie cutters for a party snack.
- Don't serve caffeinated pop for children's parties. Try our **Fizzy Fruit Drink** instead.
- Hire a teen to help you prepare and give birthday parties.
- Be careful with balloons and young children. Biting or chewing on a balloon can cause it to pop. The pressure from the air can force the rubber into a child's throat, causing choking.

Other Special Times Ideas

- Holidays can be busy times. Make it easy on yourself so you can enjoy the time with your family. Discuss with your spouse what traditions are most important to the two of you. You may be able to eliminate some time-consuming activities that don't mean as much to you.
- Consider starting a tradition of a simple Christmas dinner so Mom and Dad can relax and enjoy the day. How about a pot of chili or spaghetti, or a buffet with cold cuts, cheeses, fresh vegetables, and fruits.
- Consider what you want your child to remember from a holiday and make that a high priority.
- Use paper plates and other disposable items to make clean up as easy as possible.
- Provide a craft or other activity to entertain children when you have a large family gathering.
- Let your child decorate paper with drawings or by gluing on greeting cards. Take it to a copy store and have it laminated to make a holiday placemat.
- When a holiday means a big gathering of family and friends, plan to have some quick and nutritious snacks for the little ones. They may not be able to wait until the main meal is ready.
- If you don't normally buy sugared cereals, the individual boxes of cereal can be a once-a-year special treat from Santa.

Chapter 9

Food for Play

Kitchen fun with common ingredients

Your kitchen is probably already stocked with the ingredients for these kitchen crafts. Not only are they easy to make, they are less expensive than the commercial products. We think our Super Scented Play Dough beats anything you can buy! It smells yummy, has vivid colors, a great texture, and stores well. Try some sensory experiments with Rubber Flub and Glop. You will be surprised by the results. We have seen everyone from three year olds to gray haired grandfathers enjoying these kitchen creations.

Budding scientists will love the Baking Soda Volcanoes and the Magic Colored Celery. Who knows where this early experience with science could lead!

So, put down plastic to protect the table and floor, or take your projects outdoors on a warm day and have fun playing with food!

Food for Play

1. Super Scented Play Dough
2. Glop
3. Rubber Flub
4. Glue
5. Bubbles
6. Fruit Prints
7. Rainbow Pasta
8. Birdseed Pinecones
9. Sugar Cube Buildings
10. Magic Colored Celery
11. Baking Soda Volcanoes
12. Tasting Game

Super Scented Play Dough

This simple to make play dough is soft, smooth, scented, and nontoxic. Kids can stir the dry ingredients and help knead the cooled dough.

1 1/4 cups flour

1/4 cup salt

1 packet unsweetened flavored soft drink mix (such as Koolaid)

1 cup boiling water

1 1/2 tablespoons vegetable oil

1. In a mixing bowl, combine flour, salt, and drink mix.
2. In a separate container, combine oil and water.
3. Make a well in the flour mixture and pour in the oil and water mixture.
4. Mix thoroughly with a large spoon.
5. On a large cutting board knead dough until it is cool. Don't use the countertop as the drink mix can stain before it is mixed into the other ingredients.
6. Play! You probably have lots of tools in the kitchen to use with the play dough such as a rolling pin and cookie cutters, a garlic press to make grass or hair, chopsticks to poke holes, etc.

Note: Store in a sealed container in the cupboard for several months. It's lifetime depends upon the amount of use and time it is left out of the container. In spite of the vibrant colors this play dough does not stain hands or most surfaces once it is thoroughly mixed.

Yield: 1 3/4 cups of fun

tot tip:

This is a good activity for sick kids who are bored with being indoors. You can throw the dough away after they play with it to avoid spreading germs.

cook's tip:

Buy cornstarch by the pound (in bins) at a discount grocery store and it is very inexpensive.

tot quote:

"When I take it out and it goops off it feels like sauce."

Glop

Punch it and it repels your hand. Touch the surface slowly and it will suck in your finger like quick sand. Cleanup is a breeze since it washes off with water.

3/4 cup water
1 3/4 cups cornstarch

1. Put water in a metal pie plate or a large plastic bowl. It should be wide enough for a child's hands.
2. Slowly add cornstarch until well blended. It will be a thick liquid paste.
3. Play!

Yield: 1 cup

Rubber Flub

Who would guess that mixing two liquids would result in something that bounces, stretches, breaks, and molds to your hands. It even picks up the ink from newsprint. Watching the chemical reaction between these ingredients is a great science lesson!

3/4 cup cold water

1 cup white glue (like Elmer's)

3/4 cup hot water (from the tap)

1 1/2 teaspoons Borax

- ***a few drops of food coloring (optional)***

1. In a small bowl, combine cold water and glue.
2. In a separate small bowl, combine hot water, Borax, and food coloring until Borax is dissolved.
3. Pour Borax mixture into glue mixture.
4. Stir until a solid forms and then squeeze until the mixture is thoroughly combined. If there is a little excess liquid, pour it off.
5. Play!
6. Store in refrigerator to prevent mold growth.

Yield: about 2 cups

cook's tip:

Borax can be found with the detergents in most grocery stores.

Glue

This soft white glue washes easily from clothes. Works great for collages and other paper art projects.

1/3 cup warm water

1 tablespoon corn syrup

1/2 teaspoon white vinegar

1/4 cup cornstarch

1/3 cup cold water

1. Mix warm water, corn syrup, and vinegar in a small sauce pan over medium heat until mixture comes to a boil.
2. In a separate measuring bowl, combine cold water and cornstarch.
3. Slowly add the cornstarch mixture to the warm mixture. Mix thoroughly.
4. Let mixture cool.
5. Use a paint brush to apply glue.

Yield: 1 cup

Bubbles

Save a trip to the store by making your own bubbles. The corn syrup makes them stronger.

2 1/2 cups water

3/4 cup liquid dishwashing detergent (Dawn works well)

1/4 cup light corn syrup

1. Mix all ingredients together and have fun!

Yield: 3 1/2 cups

tot quote:

"I like to see them float."

Fruit Prints

Preschoolers will love to make creative designs with ordinary foods.

- ***oranges, lemons or apples, cut in half***
- ***nontoxic, washable liquid paint***
- ***disposable bowls***

1. Put plastic over the table and have kids wear protective aprons.
2. Place fruits on table and pour paint into small shallow bowls.
3. Dip fruit into paint and stamp on paper. You can also use leaves, carrots, corn on the cob, potatoes (can carve shapes in potatoes), etc.

tot tip:

Have kids make their own wrapping paper or decorate paper gift bags.

tot tip:

When making necklaces tape one end of the string to the table so pasta does not slide off of the yarn.

Rainbow Pasta

An adult should dye the pasta. Kids can use it to make necklaces, bracelets, crowns, and other projects.

- ***rubber gloves***
- ***disposable bowl with lid***

1 tablespoon rubbing alcohol

12-14 drops of food coloring

1 cup uncooked pasta, such as tubes or macaroni

- ***yarn***

1. Do first steps without kid's help. Food colorings will stain while wet and alcohol is dangerous. Once the alcohol has dried it is not toxic.
2. Put on rubber gloves. Place alcohol and food coloring into a small bowl.
3. Mix with a plastic spoon.
4. Add half of the pasta, put lid on bowl and shake to color pasta.
5. Scoop pasta out onto wax paper or newspaper. Repeat for the rest of the pasta.
6. Let dry overnight. Keep out of children's reach until dry.
7. Let kids string pasta onto yarn to make necklaces or bracelets. Wrap tape around one end so it is stiff, for easier threading. Colored pasta can also be glued onto paper crowns.

Yield: 1 cup

Birdseed Pinecones

Teach appreciation of nature by fixing lunch for feathered friends.

- ***pine cones***
- ***peanut butter***
- ***birdseed***

1. Spread peanut butter on pinecones.
2. Roll pinecones in birdseed.
3. Tie a string onto each pinecone
4. Hang them on a tree outside and watch for birds!

tot quote:

"I did two tall things and then a bridge."

Sugar Cube Buildings

Create a house, castle, igloo ... the possibilities are endless.

- ***white sugar cubes***
- ***liquid white glue (such as Elmer's)***
- ***paper plate or cardboard***

1. Glue sugar cubes to plate as a base and then build from there.
2. Continue gluing on cubes to build a house or castle.

To make an igloo:

1. Blow up a balloon to the size of an orange to use as the mold.
2. To form the base of the igloo, glue sugar cubes onto the plate making a ring around the balloon. Glue additional cubes onto the ring, using the balloon as a guide. Continue gluing sugar cubes to each other until the balloon is covered.
3. Let the glue dry overnight then pop the balloon.

Magic Colored Celery

Learn how plants drink water by watching the celery leaves turn color.

- ***water***
- ***red or blue food coloring***
- ***small stalk of celery—choose one that has a lot of leaves***

1. Put about 1 inch of water into a clear drinking glass or jar.
2. Add 10–12 drops of food coloring.
3. Stand celery stalk up in the water.
4. Check every few hours to see what happens.

tot quote:

"I didn't think it would work and then I just saw it."

Baking Soda Volcanoes

Try this fun science experiment for a rainy day activity.

3 tablespoons baking soda
- ***red food coloring***
- ***vinegar***

1 clear plastic cup (or cut neck off of plastic bottle)

1. Place baking soda inside cup.
2. Add a few drops of red food coloring.
3. Pour vinegar into cup until volcano *erupts*.

Tasting Game

Let preschoolers guess what they are eating with this game. They might even find something new that they like.

- ***lemon slice***
- ***orange slice***
- ***sugar cube***
- ***applesauce***
- ***ketchup***
- ***salt***
- ***cinnamon sugar***
- ***dill pickle***
- ***sweet pickle***
- ***crackers***
- ***cereals***
- ***jam***
- ***yogurt***
- ***other foods—avoid foods that can cause choking or that are too spicy***

1. Have children take turns wearing a blindfold or closing their eyes.
2. Offer some of the above foods to smell, feel, or taste and see how many each child can identify.
3. It's more fun if there are a variety of sweet, salty, and sour flavors.

variations:

Have children plug their noses and see if they can tell the difference between foods such as a slice of apple and a slice of raw potato.

tot quote:

"It's silly when you lick a lemon."

Other Food for Play Ideas

- Keep some plastic containers, wooden spoons, etc in a bottom drawer or cupboard for your toddler to play "*cooking*" while you are working in the kitchen.
- Put small food items such as O-shaped cereals or goldfish crackers into each section of a muffin pan, an empty egg carton, or an empty ice cube tray. Help your child put one in the first section, two in the next, etc. then eat them.
- Glue colored pasta, shaped cereals, and a variety of dried legumes to construction paper or cardboard to make pictures. Be sure to supervise so the beans all end up on the picture and not in a nose or ear!
- Make a placemat with outlines of a plate, cup and eating utensils. This can be used as a pattern to help a child learn how to set the table. If you laminate it with clear self-adherent plastic it is reusable.
- Make a placemat like above and cut the shapes of the dishes and utensils out of contrasting colored paper. Let your child use a glue stick to glue them on the right places on the placemat.
- Go through old magazines and cut out pictures of foods. Let your child glue pictures of favorite foods onto construction paper or cardboard.
- Choose a letter for the day and have as many foods as you can think of that start with that letter.

Section 2

Nutrition

Chapter 10

Feeding Baby

What to feed in that important first year.

During the first year of life, your baby triples in weight. Head circumference and body length increase. Vital brain functions develop. Your helpless newborn eventually learns to laugh, sit, crawl, stand, and walk. You may even hear that newsworthy first word.

All of this activity takes a lot of energy. Get your little one off to a good start by providing good nutrition during this important first year.

Feeding Baby

The First Six Months

Got Milk?

What about Cow's Milk Allergy?

Water

Vitamins, Fluoride, and Iron

Starting Solids

Six to Eight Months

Just Look at Me Now!

Moving Right Along

How Much to Feed Baby

Make Your Own Baby Foods

Commercial Baby Foods

Drinking from a Cup

Eight to Twelve Months

Finger Foods

Examples of Finger Foods

No-No's—Avoid These Foods

What's Next?

Infant Feeding Chart

The First Six Months

Got Milk?

Breast milk or iron-fortified infant formula should provide most of the nutrition for infants from birth to six months of age. Breast milk is strongly recommended. Not only is breast milk easier to digest, it provides antibodies against disease. What's more, the flavor of breast milk varies with the mother's diet so babies get used to a variety of flavors, helping them adapt to new foods later.

Breastfeeding is also good for a mother's health. Women who breastfeed recover more rapidly from childbirth and lower their lifetime risk of breast cancer. It is ideal to breastfeed your baby for at least one year.

Keep in mind that anything you eat, drink, take in pill form, or smoke, may pass through your breast milk and affect your baby. If you must take medication, check with your doctor or pharmacist about its safety for your child. Even herbal remedies can pass into breast milk and may affect your baby.

If you need help getting started with breastfeeding, there is a lot of assistance available. You can ask your pediatrician for advice. Many hospitals have nursery nurses, lactation specialists, or registered dietitians who can help you. La Leche League is also a great resource.

If it is not possible to breastfeed, consult your doctor for a formula recommendation. Most infants who are not breastfed will thrive on a cow's milk infant formula. Those with lactose intolerance can be fed a lactose-free cow's milk formula or a soy formula. Regular cow's milk, powdered milk, condensed milk, or goat's milk should not be given during the first year of life. Never give a child of any age unpasteurized milk or milk products.

What about Cow's Milk Allergy?

Most infant formulas are based on cow's milk. Fortunately, allergies to cow's milk and other foods are not very common. Symptoms of food allergy include hives and other rashes, wheezing, runny nose, vomiting, and diarrhea. If you think your baby might be allergic to milk talk to your pediatrician. Infants who develop cow's milk allergies may need further processed formulas that are designed to be less allergenic. Some milk-allergic babies can tolerate infant soy formula, but many of them are also allergic to soy.

Breastfeeding helps to prevent food allergies but doesn't completely eliminate them. Foods in a mother's diet may affect her infant. Sometimes eliminating cow's milk or other foods from a breastfeeding mother's diet will help a baby with colic or eczema. If you feel that a food in your diet is affecting your baby make sure you talk to your doctor before making any changes. See the Food and Health chapter for more information about food allergies.

Water

Breastfed and bottle-fed babies usually don't need additional water. In fact, too much water can be dangerous for an infant. When mixing formula for an infant younger than two months of age, it is a good idea to sterilize the water by boiling it for a minute or two to remove any harmful bacteria. Boiling water for longer periods of time can actually be harmful as part of the water evaporates and the minerals may become too concentrated. Bottled water is not necessarily sterile and should also be boiled for infants of this age, or you may use ready-to-feed formula. Whatever formula you use be sure to accurately follow the mixing directions.

Vitamins, Fluoride, and Iron

If you are breastfeeding, be sure to eat a healthy diet and drink plenty of fluids. Ask your doctor whether you need to take vitamins to help ensure that your milk contains what your baby needs. (If you are a vegetarian or are following any kind of a restricted diet consult a registered dietitian for advice. Your baby may need a supplement of vitamin B-12.) Breast milk contains very little vitamin D. Infants who are being completely breastfed should have a daily supplement of vitamin D. If you give your baby one bottle or more of formula a day the supplement is not necessary. Talk to your baby's doctor if you have any questions. Fluoride supplements are not necessary for the first six months of life. After six months of age, breastfed babies and formula-fed babies should receive a fluoride supplement if the drinking water does not contain fluoride. Most bottled water does not contain fluoride.

Iron is vital for a baby's brain development. Be sure to give your bottle-fed baby a formula that contains iron. There is no evidence at all that the small amount of iron in formula causes constipation. Breast milk contains enough iron for the first four to six months. After that age most breastfed babies need a source of iron in their diets. Iron-fortified infant rice cereal is the best way to provide the needed amount.

Starting Solids

At some time between four and six months of age your baby will be ready to start sampling solid foods. Solids should not be started before four months of age. At younger ages a baby's digestive tract is not ready for them. If you have a strong family history of allergy you may want to wait until your baby is six months of age. There is no reason to rush things. Solids do not help babies sleep through the night.

How do you know when your baby is ready for solids? In addition to being at least four months old, babies should have doubled their birth weights *and* weigh at least 13 pounds. They need to be able to sit well with support, maintaining their head and trunk support. They should be showing an interest in food, reaching toward objects, and opening their mouths for the spoon.

Before babies are ready for solids they need to lose their *tongue thrust reflex.* This refers to the tendency young infants have to stick their tongues out when a spoon is touched to their mouths. Babies should also be able to indicate when they are full by turning away from the spoon, closing their mouths or crying.

So, when your baby is ready for solids where do you start? An ideal first food is infant rice cereal diluted with breast milk, formula, or water to about the consistency of thick cream. Cereal is easy to digest and provides some iron, which is essential to prevent anemia. Spoon-feed cereal rather than putting it in a bottle. Part of the reason to start solid foods is to help an infant develop the ability to eat from a spoon.

Start by offering one or two teaspoons of cereal and gradually increase to as much as one to two tablespoonfuls. The cereal can be offered either before or after a milk feeding depending upon what works best with your baby. Some babies will breast or bottle feed to take the edge off of their hunger, eat their cereal, then finish with the rest of their milk. Babies are more receptive to solids when they are not overtired or overly hungry.

Six to Eight Months

Just Look at Me Now!

During the second half of the first year, your baby will be cutting teeth, improving motor skills, and developing hand-eye coordination. At this stage, babies learn to sit well without support. They are very oral and almost everything they grab goes right to their mouths. The ability to chew begins to develop and soon they are ready for new eating experiences.

Moving Right Along

When your baby is consistently eating cereal once or twice a day, you can introduce other strained or puréed foods. There are no hard and fast rules about the order of adding new foods. It doesn't matter whether you start with fruits or vegetables. The most important thing to know is that you should only give one new food at a time. For example, you might try strained carrots for three to five days, then try applesauce for a few days, then green peas. Don't give any mixed foods until you've introduced each of the ingredients separately. That way, if your baby has an allergic reaction, you will be able to easily determine which food caused the problem.

If your baby makes a face or spits out a food just try it again a week or two later. Making a face may not mean your baby doesn't like a food, but may just be a reaction to the new taste. Babies may need to taste a new food eight to ten times or more before they accept it.

How Much to Feed Baby

The main purpose of solids at this tender age is to give babies some experience with tastes and textures and with swallowing of solids. Breast milk or formula should still provide most of their nutrition. See the chart at the end of this chapter for approximate quantities needed during the first year of life. Babies' appetites vary, so don't try to force your baby to eat the quantities listed. If your baby is growing well, your baby is getting enough. Babies who are growing rapidly or who are very active may take more milk or solids than indicated in the chart.

When babies lose interest in a feeding, turn their heads away, push away, or verbally protest, it is time to stop the feeding. Don't try to force a baby to eat more just to finish a bottle or a jar of food. Let your baby's appetite determine how much is eaten.

At about seven to eight months of age your baby will probably be ready to eat three meals a day. Babies who can sit in a high chair can join the family for meals and gradually begin to eat on the family's schedule. They need breast milk or formula in between meals.

Make Your Own Baby Foods

While commercially prepared infant foods are nutritious, it is economical and easy to make your own. Just follow these simple directions:

- Make sure your hands, cooking utensils, and cooking surfaces are clean.
- Wash and peel fruits and vegetables and remove any seeds.
- Cut food into cubes and microwave, bake, or steam until tender.
- Cook meats, fish, and egg yolks thoroughly. (Note: These foods can be introduced around 8–10 months.)
- Remove bones from meats and fish.
- Purée food in a blender or baby food grinder. Add water or formula as needed.
- Don't add any salt, sugar, or spices.
- Mash ripe raw bananas for spoon-feeding.
- Mashed cooked apples or other fruits for spoon-feeding.
- Serve food at body temperature or cooler, never hot!

Be sure to use any food prepared this way within two or three days or store it in the freezer for as long as one month. Just fill ice cube trays with puree, cover with plastic wrap and freeze. When the food has frozen, remove the cubes and seal them in a plastic freezer bag. Label with the date and put the bag back in the freezer. You can also put the amount of food your child typically eats directly into a resealable plastic freezer bag, label it with the date, and put it into the freezer. When you are ready to use the food take it out and put it into the refrigerator or microwave to thaw. Don't thaw it at room temperature. Harmful bacteria can grow in food at room temperature.

Avoid home-prepared spinach, beets, turnips, carrots, and collard greens for the first few months of solid feeding. These foods contain nitrates, which can be harmful to infants. Commercial infant foods are safe as the nitrates are removed.

If you decide to make the majority of your baby's food at home, you should still use commercial iron-fortified infant cereal. It is an important source of iron for your little one.

Commercial Baby Foods

Commercial baby foods are safe and nutritious for infants. The additional cost may be worth it since the foods are ready to eat and take less of a parent's time to prepare. Tests have shown that the tiny amounts of pesticide residues found in some baby foods are usually less than that found in fresh produce. Unless you are regularly preparing a variety of fruits and vegetables that can be puréed for your baby, commercial baby foods may offer your baby more variety.

Whether to buy organic infant foods is up to you. The amount of pesticide residue in organic and nonorganic products is very similar. The cost of organic baby food is higher than nonorganic. Organic foods are grown with little or no use of pesticides so may be easier on the environment.

It is not necessary to heat the food. Room temperature is fine. Never use baby food that has passed its expiration date. If your baby will not be eating the whole jar of food spoon some into a bowl to feed from. Never put the leftovers back into the jar. If you feed your baby from the jar throw away the uneaten portion. Bacteria and enzymes from baby's saliva can cause the food to spoil.

When taking either homemade or opened jars of commercial baby food away from home carry them in a cooler or insulated bag with a cold pack. If the food gets warm discard it. Infants are especially vulnerable to food poisoning because of their immature immune systems.

Drinking From a Cup

By six to eight months of age many babies are ready to experiment with a cup. The two-handled, nonspill type of child's cup is perfect for these first attempts. Putting water in the cup helps to prevent sticky messes until your child is more experienced. It also teaches that water is an acceptable beverage.

You can also offer diluted noncitrus juice from a cup but limit the amount to no more than one or two ounces daily. Some babies and toddlers have such a sweet tooth that they will drink large quantities of juice. They may take in so many calories that they won't drink enough milk or eat enough of other foods. Juice can also cause gassiness and diarrhea in some little ones. Offer juice **only** in a cup. Sucking on juice in a bottle and holding the sweetened liquid in the mouth can cause *nursing bottle tooth decay*.

Eight to Twelve Months

Many of the foods the rest of the family eats can be offered to a baby who is eight or nine months of age or older. The textures of foods can be a little lumpier but still should be soft enough that babies can *gum* the food safely without choking. Mash or purée the food to a consistency your baby can handle. Babies at this age can have some yogurt, cheese, cottage cheese, or puddings, but should not be drinking cow's milk. Their digestive tracts are not ready to properly digest milk. Cow's milk can cause intestinal bleeding and anemia in infants less than one year old.

Finger Foods

Some time after seven or eight months, babies will begin trying to feed themselves. They are ready for finger foods when they can sit alone, can grasp food with their hands, and can get it into their mouths. Any food that holds together enough for a baby to scoop it up and get it into the mouth is a finger food. Finger foods should dissolve easily to prevent choking. Be cautious when giving baby biscuits or crackers, as a large piece can be broken off. Always supervise when your baby is eating.

Your baby might like to have a spoon to practice with while you are doing the actual feeding. Some babies older than about eight or nine months of age will not allow anyone to spoon-feed them. If this is true for your little cherub, don't try to force the issue. Instead, give foods that stick together enough to be scooped up. You can also try offering baby food spread on bread or crackers. Self-feeding is messy. Spread out a plastic sheet under the high chair to make clean up a little easier, then enjoy the show, with its resulting growth in coordination and independence.

Initially babies pick up food with the *palmar grasp*. They put their hand around an object and close their fingers over it. When they develop the *pincer grasp* and can pick up objects between thumb and finger they may be ready for smaller pieces of food.

Examples of Finger Foods for babies with *palmar grasp*

- Teething biscuits or arrowroot cookies
- Toast
- Graham crackers
- Vanilla wafers and similar cookies
- Mashed cooked vegetables such as squash, carrots, yams, potatoes

Examples of Finger Foods for babies with *pincer grasp*

- Cooked pasta
- Sliced or cubed cheese

- Cooked diced carrots
- Pieces of soft ripe banana
- No-salt-added canned vegetables
- Legumes (cooked soft enough that they are not a choking hazard)
- Dry O-shaped cereals
- Pieces of soft canned fruit, such as pear or peach
- Avocado
- Cottage cheese
- Very tender finely chopped chicken
- Well-cooked ground meat
- Soft fish with the bones removed

Some Finger Food Recipes in this book:

Choose from this list and modify them as necessary. For example, some may need to be cut up into bite-sized pieces.

- Apple Crisp Muffins
- Applesauce Gel Squares
- Baby's First Cookie
- Baby's First Cake
- Baked Fries
- Baked Potato Bar
- Banana Cookies
- Banana Cupcakes
- Cheezy Pretzels
- Fruity Jigglers
- Hawaiian Muffins
- Mac 'n' Cheese
- Mixer Meatloaf
- Poached Pears
- Prune Muffins
- Refrigerator Bran Muffins

- Sweet Potato Muffins
- Twisty Pasta Salad
- Whole Wheat Pancakes
- Yogurt Cheese spread on bread
- Zucchini Quesadillas

No-No's—Avoid These Foods During the First Year of Life

- Honey–risk of botulism. Processed foods, such as honey graham crackers are safe
- Cow's milk, including powdered or condensed milk–not digested well, can cause intestinal bleeding and anemia
- Goat's milk–poorly digested, not nutritionally complete, potential allergy
- Soy milk (unless it is soy infant formula) or rice milk–incomplete nutrition
- Unpasteurized juices or milk–can cause food poisoning
- Grapes, hot dogs, nuts and seeds, popcorn, raw vegetables, raisins, hard candies, chunks of solid foods–choking hazards
- Peanut butter–potential allergy, choking hazard
- Egg whites–potential allergy
- Wheat–avoid if strong family history of allergy
- Citrus fruits, citrus fruit juice, tomatoes and tomato juice–potential allergy
- Shellfish–potential allergy
- Artificial sweeteners and colorings–not necessary and potentially harmful
- Carbonated beverages–no nutrition, can cause gassiness
- Candy–decreases appetite for more nourishing foods and may cause tooth decay, choking hazard

- Chocolate –decreases appetite for more nourishing foods and contains caffeine
- Caffeine, such as cola drinks, tea, or coffee–can cause irritability, breast-feeding mothers should avoid excess caffeine
- Added salt or seasonings–unnecessary, may be linked to later high blood pressure
- Excessive amounts of high fiber foods–may interfere with absorption of important nutrients
- Alcohol–toxic to developing brain, breastfeeding mothers should avoid

What's Next?

As your baby approaches the second year, gradually increase the amount of solid foods given and begin to wean from the breast or bottle. The goal is to completely wean from the bottle by twelve to fifteen months of age and to reduce breastfeeding frequency. If you continue breastfeeding beyond twelve months of age, make sure to also give an adequate amount of solids to provide the variety of nutrients, flavors, and textures your baby needs.

At twelve months of age, whole cow's milk can be gradually introduced. Encourage your baby to experiment more and more with finger foods and with handling a spoon. See the chapter on **Nutrition for Your Growing Child** for more detailed information about what your child needs after one year of age.

Infant Feeding Chart

If your infant is premature, developmentally delayed, or allergic, consult your pediatrician

Foods	Readiness signs	0–4 months	4–6 months
Breast Milk or Formula, other Dairy Foods	Can suck & swallow	About 16–32 ounces breast milk or formula daily	About 24–40 ounces breast milk or formula daily
Water	Able to hold cup	None	None
Fluoride	N/A	None	None
Vitamins	N/A	Yes, if breastfed	Yes, if breastfed
Juice	Able to hold cup 6 months or older	None	None
Grains	4 months or older, double birth weight, and over 13 pounds Sits with support, opens mouth for spoon	None	(Optional) infant rice cereal, 1–2 teaspoons up to 1–2 tablespoons once or twice daily
Fruits & Vegetables	Tolerating cereal Interested in more	None	None
Protein Foods	Tolerating cereal, variety of fruits & vegetables Reducing milk intake	None	None
Finger Foods	Sits alone, bites, chews Palmar or pincer grasp	None	None

6–8 months	**8–10 months**	**10--12 months**
About 24–40 ounces breast milk or formula daily	About 24–40 ounces breast milk or formula, yogurt, cheese daily	20–32 ounces breast milk or formula, yogurt, cheese daily
Sips in cup if taking other foods well	Sips in cup if taking other foods well	1–2 ounces in cup
Yes, if water does not contain fluoride	Yes, if water does not contain fluoride	Yes, if water does not contain fluoride
Yes, if breastfed	Yes, if breastfed	Yes, if breastfed
(Optional) 1–2 ounces diluted noncitrus juice in cup	(Optional) 2–4 ounces diluted noncitrus juice in cup	(Optional) 2–4 ounces diluted noncitrus juice in cup
Infant rice cereal, gradually try other varieties of infant cereal 3–4 tablespoons once or twice daily	Infant cereals 3–4 tablespoons once or twice daily Pasta, rice, teething biscuits if ready for finger foods	Infant cereals 3–4 tablespoons once or twice daily Bread, bagels, muffins, crackers
Stage 1 or homemade 1–3 tablespoons once or twice daily	Stage 2 or finely chopped table foods, 2–4 tablespoons two to three times daily	Stage 3 or table foods 3–4 tablespoons two or three times daily
None	Strained or chopped meats, egg yolk, or legumes, 1–2 teaspoons up to 2–3 tablespoons daily	Casseroles, finely chopped or ground meats, quantity according to appetite 2–4 tablespoons daily
Teething biscuits if sits and grasps food Be careful of choking	Pincer grasp foods, some spoon self-feeding Be careful of choking	Expanded variety of finger foods, spoon foods Be careful of choking

Chapter 11

Nutrition for Your Growing Child

From baby food to family meals

Once your child has outgrown puréed food, what's next? Recent studies indicate that most children have diets that need improvement. The quality of a child's diet often declines between the ages of two and six years of age. Feeding a toddler doesn't have to be complicated. This nutritional guide provides the information you need to assure that your child is getting the basics.

The Food Group Pyramid is an excellent source for planning a balanced diet for toddlers and preschoolers. There are enough choices in each food group to satisfy the most difficult-to-please eaters, especially if you use our picky eater tips. Don't worry if your child doesn't eat all of the recommended foods every day. Watching eating patterns over a week or two is a better way to judge your child's diet. To see the results of all this good nutrition, plot your child's height and weight on the growth charts provided in the Appendix.

Nutrition for Your Growing Child

Food Group Pyramid

Food Group Guidelines Ages 1–6

Calorie Requirements

Grains

Vegetables

Fruits

Dairy Products

Meats & Other Protein

Fats & Sweets

Vegetarian Diets

Nutrition Facts

Carbohydrates

Fats

Fiber

Protein

Minerals

Vitamins

Supplements

Food Additives

Natural and Organic Foods

Mineral Chart

Vitamin Chart

Food Group Pyramid

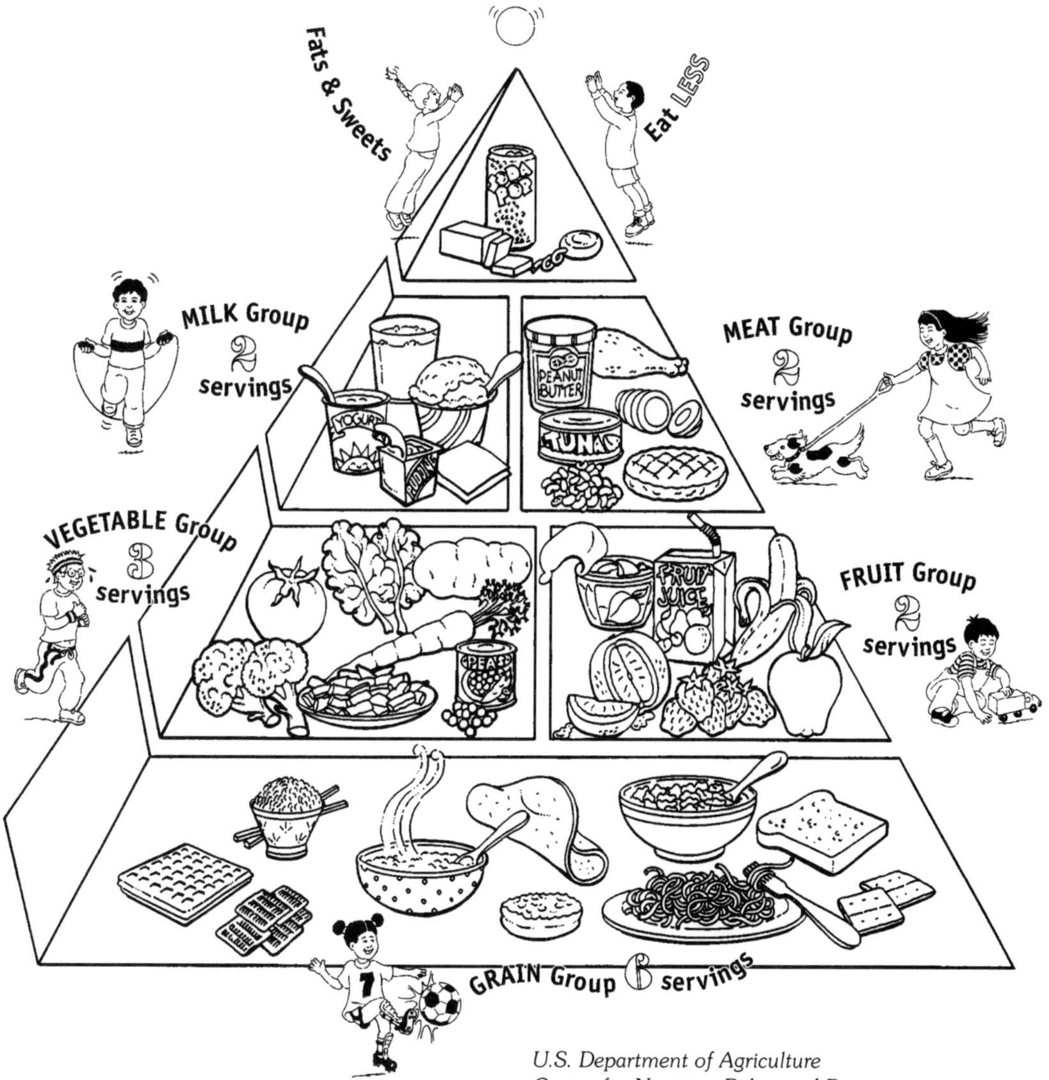

U.S. Department of Agriculture
Center for Nutrition Policy and Promotion
January 2000, Program Aid 1651

Food Group Guidelines Ages 1–6

Using the Food Group Pyramid, this chapter provides guidelines to help you understand your child's nutritional needs. You will notice that serving sizes for children are quite small. A serving for a preschooler is about one-fourth to one-half of an adult serving. **One tablespoon of food per year of age is a typical serving.** The serving sizes don't necessarily reflect the amount children eat at one time. For example, rather than drinking one cup of milk a child might take several smaller servings of milk, cheese, or yogurt over the course of a day.

Calorie Requirements

- *Approximately* 1,000 calories per day for the first year of life, 100 more calories for every additional year. A five-year-old will need about 1,400 calories.
- Don't worry about counting calories. The number your child needs depends upon activity level and growth rate. A large, active child needs more calories than one who is smaller or less active.
- If your child is growing well and is healthy the calorie intake is fine. If a child is gaining weight too rapidly the calorie intake may be excessive. If your child is not healthy and growing normally, consult your pediatrician or a pediatric registered dietitian.

Calorie content of foods

- One gram of fat provides 9 calories
- One gram of protein or carbohydrate provides 4 calories

GRAINS—6 or more servings/day

Food choices: Breads, crackers, cereals, pasta, rice, muffins, pancakes, bagels, cookies.

Serving size:

- **Ages 1–3:** 1/4–1/2 slice bread; 1–3 tablespoons cooked rice, pasta, cereals; 1–2 graham cracker squares; 2–3 whole-grain crackers; 1/2–1 small roll, pancake, waffle, biscuit, or muffin.
- **Ages 4–6:** 1/2–1 slice bread; 4–6 tablespoons cooked rice, pasta, or cereal; 2–3 graham cracker squares; 3–4 whole-grain crackers; 1/3 cup ready-to-eat cereal; 3 cups popped popcorn*; 1 flour or corn tortilla; 1 small roll, pancake, waffle, biscuit, or muffin.

Picky eater tips: Not usually a problem; children typically like these foods.

Too much: These foods are filling and may suppress the appetite for protein foods, fruits, and vegetables. Too much fiber may cause diarrhea.

* *Possible choking hazard*

VEGETABLES—3 to 5 servings/day

Food choices: Fresh, frozen, canned, or cooked vegetables; vegetable juices. Deeply colored yellow and green vegetables have the highest vitamin content.

Serving size:

- **Ages 1–3:** 1–3 tablespoons raw* or cooked vegetables; 1/4 cup vegetable juice; 1/4 cup spaghetti sauce.
- **Ages 4–6:** 1/4–1/2 cup raw* or cooked vegetables; 1/3 cup vegetable juice; 1/2 cup spaghetti sauce; 1/2–1 medium carrot*; 1/2–1 cup leafy raw vegetables.

Picky eater tips: Add grated, chopped or pureed vegetables to soups, muffins, breads, cookies, pancakes, sandwiches, casseroles, spaghetti sauce, etc. Serve cooked vegetables with a little cheese sauce, butter, or catsup. Try raw* or steamed vegetables with dips. Try Asian style stir-fried vegetables. Don't give up–keep offering vegetables and your child will develop a taste for them. In the meantime, offer vitamin-rich fruits, such as cantaloupe, nectarines, peaches, plums, apricots, and berries as substitutes for vegetables.

Too much: Not a common problem! Only one in five American children eat enough vegetables. Most vegetables are low in iron, protein, fat, and calories so vegetarian diets need to be carefully planned to meet a young child's needs. Carotenemia, a harmless yellow staining of the skin, can occur if a child eats large amounts of yellow and orange vegetables such as carrots, squash, and sweet potatoes.

**Possible choking hazards*

FRUITS—2 to 4 servings/day

Food choices: Fresh, frozen, canned, or dried fruits; fruit purées, 100% fruit leathers, fruit juices.

Serving size:

- **Ages 1–3:** 1/4 medium apple, pear, banana, or peach; 1–3 tablespoons applesauce or other canned fruit; 1–3 tablespoons berries*; 1–2 tablespoons dried fruit* or equivalent amount of 100% fruit leather; 1–2 ounces 100% fruit juice.
- **Ages 4–6:** 1/2–1 medium apple, pear, orange*, banana, or peach; 1/4–1/2 cup applesauce or other canned fruit; 1/4–1/2 cup berries; 1/4 cup dried fruit or equivalent amount of 100% fruit leather; 2–4 ounces 100% fruit juice.

Picky eater tips: Offer dried fruits* or 100% fruit leather. Add fruit to muffins, cookies, cakes, gelatins, puddings, etc. Mix fruit with yogurt or milk to make a smoothie. Top cereal or pancakes with fruit. Offer fruit for snacks and desserts.

Too much: Limit juice to 4 ounces a day. Excess juice can cause diarrhea and can reduce appetite for other foods. Use 100% juice—juice drinks are watered down with added sugars, flavorings, and colorings. Large amounts of high fiber fruits can cause diarrhea. If your child gets diarrhea from normal amounts of fruit and juice, consult your pediatrician about fructose intolerance.

**Possible choking hazards*

DAIRY PRODUCTS—2 to 3 servings/day

Food choices: Whole milk until two years of age. After two years of age use 2%, 1% or fat free milk. Yogurt, cheese, cottage cheese, ice cream, puddings, and soups made with milk. If your child has a *proven* allergy to cow's milk be sure the diet includes calcium and vitamin D from other sources.

Serving size:

- **Ages 1–3:** 1/2–2/3 cup milk, yogurt, or calcium-fortified soy milk; 1/2–1 ounce cheese; 1/2–1 string cheese; 1/2 cup frozen yogurt or pudding.
- **Ages 4–6:** 1 cup milk, yogurt, or calcium fortified soy milk; 1–1 1/2 ounces cheese; 1 string cheese counts as 2/3 of a milk serving. 1 cup frozen yogurt or pudding; 1/2 cup of ice cream counts as 1/3 of a milk serving.

Picky eater tips: Young children often prefer milk at room temperature. Offer milk at every meal and limit juice. Use milk instead of water when cooking oatmeal and other cereals. Add powdered milk to pancakes, muffins, and other baked foods: two tablespoons of powdered milk for every cup of flour. Make fruit smoothies with milk or yogurt and fruit. Put milk in a special cup or offer a straw. Offer flavored milk such as chocolate. Use cheese sauce on vegetables. Make creamed soups or casseroles. Try calcium-enriched soy milk, rice milk, or orange juice.

Too much: Excessive milk can reduce a child's appetite for other important foods. Milk contains no iron so drinking too much milk can cause anemia.

MEATS & OTHER PROTEIN–2 to 3 servings/day

Food Choices: Cooked dried peas, beans, and lentils; peanut butter*, eggs, tofu, lean red meat, poultry, fish, canned tuna, lowfat luncheon meats, hot dogs.**

Serving size:

- **Ages 1–3:** 1 ounce (about 4 tablespoons or 1/4 cup) cooked lean meat, poultry, fish or tofu; 1/2 egg; 1–2 tablespoons peanut butter*; 1/4 cup tuna; 1–3 tablespoons legumes; 1/2–1 soy burger; 1–2 slices lunch meat; 1/2–1 hot dog.**
- **Ages 4–6:** 1–2 ounces (about 1/4–1/2 cup) cooked lean meat, poultry, fish or tofu; 1 egg; 2 tablespoons peanut butter*; 1/4 cup tuna; 1/2 cup legumes; 1 soy burger patty; 2 slices lean lunchmeat; 1–2 hot dogs.**

Picky eater tips: Add legumes or ground or chopped meat to soups, sauces, casseroles, etc. Strained commercial baby food meats can be spread on bread or crackers as a sandwich. Offer peanut butter in dips for raw or steamed vegetables and fruits. Offer peeled and sliced hard-boiled eggs.

Too much: Some of these foods are relatively high in fat so they should not be overused.

**Possible choking hazard unless spread thinly or mixed with honey or jam.*

*** Possible choking hazard, also high in fat, salt, and additives—use infrequently.*

FATS & SWEETS—use sparingly

Food Choices: Oils, margarine, butter, salad dressing, chips, doughnuts, jam and jelly, honey, candy, soft drinks, fruit snacks, store-bought cookies.

Serving size:

Fats should be used sparingly after age 2. Children younger than 2 years of age need to get about 50% of their calories from fat for normal growth and brain development. Sweets should be offered sparingly at any age.

Picky eater tips: Not applicable.

Too much: These foods typically supply calories without a lot of nutrition. The sugary foods can contribute to dental caries. Too much of these foods can lead to obesity and other health problems.

A note about sugar: Think sugar causes hyperactivity? Children have actually been found to be calmer after having sugar! Sugar increases serotonin, a brain chemical that has a calming effect. The common belief that sugar causes hyperactivity may be explained by the fact that sweets are often given for special occasions such as birthday parties. The excitement of the activity may be the cause of the behavior.

Vegetarian Diets

Many families are beginning to choose vegetarian diets. A vegetarian diet is generally lower in fat and calories and higher in fiber than a meat-based diet. This may result in lower cholesterol levels and less obesity, heart disease and cancer. However, a vegetarian diet needs to be carefully planned to provide enough protein, fat, iron, vitamin B12, calcium, zinc, and calories to meet the needs of a growing child. The amount of food required to obtain these nutrients may be more than a child can eat. A consultation with a registered dietitian is a good investment if you are planning to feed your child a vegetarian diet. It may be necessary to learn new cooking techniques to prepare alternative protein sources such as legumes and soy.

Types of vegetarian diets:

- Partial–includes everything except red meat.
- Lacto-ovo-vegetarian–includes eggs and milk, no fish, poultry, or red meat.
- Lacto-vegetarian–includes milk, no eggs, fish, poultry, or red meat.
- Ovo-vegetarian–includes eggs, no milk, fish, poultry, or red meat.
- Vegan–no eggs, milk products, fish, poultry, or red meat.

Nutrition Facts

Foods are made up of a variety of substances that are important for body growth and functioning. Some of the most important are carbohydrates, fats, fiber, protein, minerals, and vitamins.

Carbohydrates

What they are: ***Complex*** carbohydrates are starches or polysaccharides. ***Simple*** carbohydrates are sugars such as lactose, sucrose, dextrose, and fructose.

What they do: Provide energy and contribute sweet flavors, bulk, and texture to foods.

How much: After infancy about 50% of calories should come from carbohydrates.

Too much: Carbohydrates are filling and can reduce the appetite for other foods. Sugars contribute to tooth decay. Too many calories can cause obesity.

Sources:

- ***Simple*** carbohydrates are found in milk and milk products, fruits, fruit juice, table sugar, honey, jam, soft drinks, candy, and other desserts.
- ***Complex*** carbohydrates are found in breads, cereals, rice, pasta, and some fruits and vegetables.

All you need to know: Choose complex carbohydrates and limit simple carbohydrates.

A note about carbonated drinks: Soft drinks are mixtures of water, sugar or artificial sweeteners, chemical flavors, and colors. They have no nutritional value. The phosphorous used in carbonation may cause calcium loss. Give soft drinks seldom, if at all, to preschool children.

Fats

What they are: Fats come in two general types: ***saturated*** and ***unsaturated***. Our bodies need both, but no more than 1/3 of the fat eaten should come from saturated fats and 2/3 from unsaturated. The amount of saturated fat in the diet affects blood cholesterol level.

***Saturated fat*:** solid at room temperature

- **Naturally saturated fats**–butter, cocoa butter, coconut oil, and the fat on meat.
- **Hydrogenated fats**–oils that have hydrogen added to make them less likely to spoil and to make them solid at room temperature. Shortening and solid margarine for example.

***Unsaturated fat*:** liquid at room temperature

- **Monounsaturated fats**–liquid at room temperature and get firmer when refrigerated. They are found in canola oil, peanut oil and olive oil.
- **Polyunsaturated fats**–liquid at room temperature or when refrigerated. These are fish oils, salad dressings, soft margarines and most vegetable oils. There is some evidence that mono-unsaturated fats may be better for us than poly-unsaturated.

What they do: Provide energy, promote brain growth in infants, and aid hormone production, blood clotting, and absorption of vitamins A,D,E, and K. Provide flavor and texture to foods.

How much:

- Birth to age 2: 50% of calories need to be from fat to provide for brain development and growth.
- Age 2 and older: gradually decrease to 30% of total calories.

Too much: Obesity, high cholesterol levels, and fatty deposits in the arteries.

Sources: Animal products such as meats, eggs, and dairy products. Also butter, margarine, oils, salad dressings, pastries, fried foods, nuts, and nut butters.

All you need to know: Be sure to feed young children enough fat for growth and brain development. Use whole milk until age two. After age two, gradually transition to lowfat or nonfat milk. Unsaturated fats are healthier than saturated or hydrogenated fats so when possible use oils rather than shortening in cooking. (Some baked goods will not have the right texture if oils are substituted for solid fats.) Prepared foods such as mixes, crackers, and cookies often have a lot of hidden fat and should not be used frequently.

A note about cholesterol: Cholesterol is found in meats, eggs, and dairy products. It isn't actually a fat but is a lipid. People of all ages need some cholesterol in their diets, but less than 300 milligrams a day.

Fiber

What it is: The part of fruits, vegetables, and grains that cannot be digested.

What it does: Provides bulk and a feeling of fullness, helps prevent overeating and obesity, and prevents constipation and appendicitis. May help prevent coronary artery disease, colon cancer, and adult-onset diabetes.

How much: Child's age plus five grams per day. For example, a two-year-old child needs 7 grams per day. Maximum is age plus 10 grams.

Too Much: Uncommon, but can interfere with absorption of calcium, zinc, iron, and trace minerals. Can result in inadequate caloric intake and poor growth. Can also cause gas, diarrhea, and abdominal discomfort.

Sources: Fruits, vegetables, cooked dried beans, split peas, and lentils. Whole grain cereals, crackers, breads, brown rice, oatmeal, oat bran, wheat bran, corn bran, popcorn*, nuts*, and nut butters*.

All you need to know: Offer your child five servings of fruits and vegetables a day. Choose whole grain cereals, crackers, and breads that list whole wheat, rye, oats, or corn as the first ingredient. Serve legumes often. If you are vegetarian be aware that high fiber foods may be so filling that a young child can't eat enough to get the nutrition needed.

**Possible choking hazards*

Protein

What it is: Chemical compounds made up of amino acids.

What it does: Provides major building blocks of body tissues, antibodies, hormones, and enzymes. Protein is also an energy source.

How much: An infant needs one gram of protein per pound of body weight each day. This gradually decreases to about half a gram per pound by age five.

Too much: Excess protein can be turned into fatty tissue. It also may have long-term harmful effects on kidney function.

Sources: Lean red meat, fish, poultry, eggs, milk, and other dairy products. Also breast milk, soy milk, tofu, wheat germ, nuts, legumes, and whole grains.

Supplements: Usually not necessary.

All you need to know: Two servings from the meat and protein group provide all that is needed. Children on vegetarian diets need high-protein foods such as legumes, soy, and whole grains.

Minerals

Minerals are chemicals required by the body in small amounts. They include calcium, chloride, fluoride, iron, magnesium, phosphorous, potassium, sodium, and zinc. Minerals have a wide variety of functions in the body including regulating fluid balance, heart rate, and enzyme functions. The most important ones are summarized in the chart at the end of this chapter.

Vitamins

Vitamins are nutrients that are essential to basic chemical functions of the body. Before their chemical structures were known, they were identified by letters of the alphabet. They now have other names, but many of them are still identified by letters.

Vitamins consist of two categories, water-soluble and fat-soluble. The water-soluble vitamins, B vitamins and vitamin C, are not stored in the body so need to be replenished daily, and are not likely to be toxic. The fat-soluble vitamins, A, D, E, and K can be stored in the fatty tissues of the body and can build up to toxic levels.

The recommended daily allowances of vitamins are so small that they are usually measured in milligrams and micrograms. Vitamin D is measured in International Units (I.U.). International Units are a measure of activity and milligrams and micrograms are measures of weight. Basic facts about vitamins are in the chart at the end of this chapter.

Supplements–Are they necessary?

Once a child is eating a variety of foods, vitamin and mineral supplements are usually not necessary and can even be harmful. There are a few exceptions. Here's what you need to know about supplements:

- Fluoride should be given to children whose drinking water is not fluoridated. This is important to tooth enamel development and prevention of tooth decay. The right amount of fluoride is not harmful. Most bottled water does not contain fluoride.
- Children who refuse to eat foods from one of the major food groups may temporarily need a supplement until they learn to eat those foods. Breastfed infants should be given vitamin D supplements. Infant formulas

contain vitamin D. Infants drinking at least one bottle of formula a day do not need a supplement.

- If your child is intolerant or allergic to important foods ask your doctor for recommendations for substitute foods or supplements. For example, a child who is not drinking milk will need other sources of vitamin D and calcium.
- Vegetarian diets may not contain enough iron or vitamin B12 for children. Consider a consultation with a registered dietitian to see if your child needs supplements.
- Children with medical problems that affect vitamin absorption may need supplements.
- Iron supplements should only be given to children who have iron deficiency anemia. Toddlers can develop anemia if they drink too much milk and eat too few iron-containing foods. Iron given unnecessarily can temporarily stain tooth enamel, cause constipation, and can be very toxic if overdosed.
- Children who are economically deprived and do not have access to healthy diets may need supplements.
- Children with disabilities that interfere with eating need evaluation by a registered dietitian and may need special formulas or supplements.
- Fiber supplements should be given only for constipation or encopresis (stool holding and bowel accidents). Talk with your pediatrician or a registered dietitian before using them on a regular basis.
- Avoid giving herbal products to children. They have not been approved by the FDA for use in children and some may have toxic effects.

Food Additives

Read the label on prepared foods and you will see ingredients such as monosodium glutamate (MSG), aspartame, vitamins, sulfites, nitrites, and caffeine. These are food additives—chemicals added to food to make it more nutritious, change its color or flavor, or keep it from spoiling. Additives can be manmade or natural. Are they safe? The answer is *usually*. Some people are allergic to sulfites or food colorings. MSG and aspartame can cause headaches and diarrhea. Some other common additives are:

- **Artificial Sweeteners:** Aspartame (NutraSweet), saccharin, acesulfame-K, xylitol, and sorbitol are chemicals often referred to as non-nutritive sweeteners. They add sweetness without calories to foods such as carbonated drinks, gum, yogurt, and other foods advertised as sugar-free. Artificial sweeteners can cause diarrhea in some people.
- **Antibiotics:** Antibiotics fed to animals can cause bacteria to become resistant so that the antibiotics will not work to treat human infections. Food irradiation is an ideal way to solve this problem.
- **Caffeine:** Caffeine is a nervous system stimulant and can cause anxiety, irritability, overactivity, wakefulness, upset stomach, increased heart rate, and irregular heart rhythm. It can also cause fluid loss which contributes to dehydration when children are active and sweating. Caffeine has not been found to stunt growth. Coffee contains 100 to 200 milligrams of caffeine per cup, tea 60 to100 milligrams, colas 30 milligrams or more per 12 ounces, cocoa about 5 milligrams per cup.
- **Food irradiation:** The use of radiation to kill harmful bacteria, insects, and molds does *not* make food radioactive and doesn't significantly change the nutritional content of food. It is a safe way to prevent serious problems such as *e. coli* poisoning.
- **Genetic engineering:** Using the genes from one food to enhance qualities of another food appears to be a safe way to increase production and hardiness of crops. Most corn and soy sold in the United States

is genetically engineered. The only known risk with this technique is for people who have allergies to a *donor* food. For example, if a gene from peanuts was used to make soybeans grow better, people who are allergic to peanuts could react to the soy.

- **Hormones:** BST (bovine somatotropin) is given to dairy cows to increase milk production. Some of the hormone shows up in the milk, but there is also BST in the milk of untreated cows. 90% of it is removed by pasteurization. The tiny amount left is digested by enzymes in the gastrointestinal tract and has no effect on the human body. BST does not change the flavor or nutrition of milk. Milk from treated cows also contains a small amount of Growth Factor which is also digested and not absorbed. There is no reason to avoid using milk from treated cows.
- **Pasteurization:** Heat treating dairy products and fruit juices to kill harmful bacteria. **Never** give a child unpasteurized milk, cheese, yogurt, or fruit juice. Unpasteurized products can cause life-threatening illnesses.

Natural and Organic Foods

- **Natural foods:** Natural food is less processed or altered from the original state. Whole wheat flour and brown rice are more natural than white flour and white rice. Natural foods usually contain more fiber and do not contain additives, but may require more preparation time. While there are sometimes more vitamins in natural foods, processed grain products are often fortified with vitamins to make them equivalent. Too much fiber in the diet can prevent absorption of vitamins. This is not usually a problem if they are part of a varied diet.
- **Organic foods:** The term *organic* describes the way the plant or animal was raised. Organic plants are fertilized with manure and compost without pesticides so they may be easier on the environment. Organic foods often spoil faster since they are untreated. They are often not entirely free of pesticides. Organic meats are from animals that have not received hormones or antibiotics.

Whether to spend the extra money on these foods depends on your budget and personal preference. Non-organic foods often have no more pesticides than organic foods and can be as nutritious and flavorful. Washing fresh fruits and vegetables thoroughly with water and removing the outer leaves of leafy vegetables removes most pesticides.

Mineral Chart

Mineral	Calcium	Fluoride	Iron	Zinc
What it does	Builds strong bones and teeth, aids normal nerve and muscle function, and aids blood clotting.	Prevents tooth decay, strengthens tooth enamel.	Prevents anemia, essential for mental development of toddlers.	Promotes growth and muscle development.
How much	1 to 3 years: 500–800 milligrams 4 to 8 years: 800–1200 milligrams	Depends on age and amount in drinking water.	10 milligrams per day	5–15 milligrams per day, depending on age
Too much	May cause kidney stones and interfere with absorption of iron. Don't exceed 2500 milligrams/ day.	Can cause discoloration of tooth enamel.	Build-up in body tissues causes damage. overdose is dangerous.	Can interfere with iron absorption.
Sources	Milk, cheese, yogurt, tofu, fortified orange juice, fortified soy or rice milk Some vegetables, legumes, and grains.	Occurs naturally in some water, may be added to city drinking water.	Iron-fortified cereals, red meat, legumes, apricots, raisins, molasses, spinach, other dark green leafy vegetables	Meat, fish, dairy products, legumes, nuts, whole-grain cereals
Supplements	For milk allergy, lactose intolerance or poor milk intake.	Recommended if not in drinking water.	Only if a child has proven anemia, too much can be harmful.	May be needed by vegetarians.
All You Need to Know	Make sure your child's diet includes the recommended number of servings of dairy products.	Be sure your drinking water is fluoridated. Bottled water does not usually contain fluoride.	A common cause of iron deficiency is excessive consumption of milk or juice. Be sure your child eats iron-containing foods every day.	Don't take supplements without consulting your doctor or dietitian.

Vitamins

Vitamin	B Vitamins	Vitamin C	Vitamin A	Vitamin D	Vitamin E	Vitamin K
What it does	Aid enzyme, metabolic, digestive, blood and nerve function. Folic acid helps prevent birth defects.	Aids iron absorption, strengthens blood vessels, may help fight infection.	Involved in growth, immune system function, and vision.	Builds healthy bones and prevents rickets by helping the body absorb calcium.	Important for healthy blood, muscles, and nervous system. May prevent heart disease and cancer.	Important in blood clotting.
How much	Varies with age and body size.	30–45 milligrams per day for preschool children	1–3 years—400 micrograms 4–6 years—500 micrograms	400 international units or 10 micrograms	3–7 milligrams	10–20 micrograms daily for preschool children
Too much	Too much of any one of the B vitamins can interfere with the absorption of the others.	Can cause diarrhea, burning with urination, and kidney stones.	Excessive supplements are toxic, even fatal.	Excessive supplements can be toxic.	May cause bleeding problems.	Toxic effects not known.
Sources	Meats, milk, fortified grains and cereals, nuts, legumes, and vegetables Vitamin B12 only in eggs, milk, and meat, not in vegetables or fruits	Citrus fruits, tomatoes, berries, dark green vegetables	Dark green & yellow vegetables; yellow & orange fruits, liver, fish oil, eggs, fortified dairy products	Added to cow's milk, infant formulas, some soy milks and rice milks. The body manufactures vitamin D when exposed to sun.	Poultry, seafood, nuts, egg yolk, green leafy vegetables, avocado, wheat germ, legumes, whole grains, vegetable oils	Made by intestinal bacteria. Leafy green vegetables, milk, pork, some grains

12 Chapter

Eating Behaviors

How to handle common eating problems

In addition to knowing *what* to feed your child, it is important to know *how* to feed your child. Have mealtimes turned into power struggles? Do you worry that your child eats too little or too much, behaves badly, or won't try new foods? Do you cook a separate meal for a child who refuses to eat what is prepared for the family? There is a better way!

Developing healthy attitudes about food starts during infancy. Children's appetites, temperaments, and developmental stages influence their eating habits. Most children go through a picky phase. If you know how to respond to difficult behavior you can get your child off to a healthy start and help prevent later eating problems.

Eating Behaviors

Why It's Normal for Young Children to Be Picky Eaters

Ages One to Three

Ages Four to Six

Seven Rules for Encouraging Healthy Eating

Solutions for Common Eating Behavior Problems

Preventing Eating Disorders

Body Image

Recognizing Body Signals of Hunger and Satiety

Attitudes about Food

Attitudes about Physical Activity

Understanding and Preventing Obesity

Causes of Obesity in Children

How to Tell if Your Child is Overweight

What to Do if Your Child is Overweight

An Ounce of Prevention May Equal a Pound of Cure

Fitness Activities

Table-Time Tips for Family Meals

Eating Out With Preschoolers

Signs of a Tot-Friendly Restaurant

What to Take with You

Safety Tips

What to Order

Encouraging Good Behavior

Why It's Normal for Young Children to Be Picky Eaters

Why is it that young children are often labeled as picky eaters? Could it be normal for them? Whenever a characteristic applies to a large number of children it might be a normal developmental phase. For example, even though it is hard on parents, newborns wake during the night and require feedings every two to three hours. Parents know that this will be a passing phase, so they cope with it. Toddlers have characteristics that make it normal for them to be picky about what they eat. Accepting that this is a phase can make it easier to handle feeding challenges.

Ages One to Three

Some characteristics of toddlers that cause them to be picky eaters:

- Slower growth rate than during the first 12 months of life, so have a natural decrease in appetite.
- Preference for routines and caution about new experiences, including new foods.
- Increased independence and discovery of own opinions, so increased resistance to parental requests.
- Enthusiasm for new-found ability to walk and run, so little willingness to sit still for long. Some toddlers may only be able to sit at the table for ten or fifteen minutes.
- Tendency to be ready for sleep when the rest of the family is ready for dinner.
- Strong desire for attention, which they may seek through difficult behavior.
- Inclination to like only one thing for awhile, then suddenly refuse that and want something different.
- Preference for food at a tepid temperature—like Goldilocks—not too hot and not too cold.

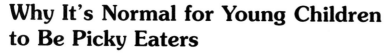

- Tendency to be overwhelmed by large servings of food, so need manageable serving sizes.
- Desire to feed themselves with their hands, so may refuse spoon-feeding.
- Small stomach capacity, so need regular meals and between-meal snacks.
- Tendency to be easily distracted so may lose interest in eating if there are other things going on.

It's not all bad; toddlers are also very interested in participating in their environment. These characteristics can help you find ways to make meals appealing to them:

- Want to imitate parents, siblings, or other children.
- Love active involvement—helping to cook, playing with toy dishes and utensils while a parent is preparing food.
- Prefer interesting-looking food—colorful, fun shapes, etc.
- Are interested in self-feeding. Can drink from cup with a lid and begin to use spoon and dull fork.
- Enjoy making choices.

Ages Four to Six

Just when you get used to their behavior, a new developmental stage begins. About age three to four some changes occur that may affect the way children eat. Some of the challenging behaviors at this age include:

- Increasingly strong preferences (sandwiches always have to be cut in half, etc.).
- Erratic appetite, very hungry one day and not at all the next.
- Increased vulnerability to television advertisements for sugared cereals and fast foods.

- Increased demands for favorite foods.
- Preference for separate foods rather than mixed, as in casseroles.
- Reversion to younger behaviors when sick, tired, or stressed.
- More interest in talking or playing than eating.

However, in general, children this age are easier to feed because of the following changes:

- Increased desire to please parents and other adults.
- Improved coordination, so can self-feed with less mess using cup, spoon, and fork.
- Ability to sit at the table for longer periods of time.
- Increased willingness to try new foods. Children this age may still prefer simple foods, but occasionally will love something unusual like artichokes or mushrooms.
- Eagerness to help with food preparation.
- Rapidly developing language skills, so improved ability to communicate preferences.
- Increased stomach capacity.
- Better table manners. They are less impulsive, so can follow directions, and can be more patient when they are hungry.
- Ability to serve themselves and pass food to others.
- New interest in eating with other children.

Now you know why it is normal for children to go through phases of being picky about their eating. While these behaviors are normal and age-appropriate, some of them turn into bad habits if not handled well. What can you do to make sure your child eats what is needed to be healthy? Keep reading to find out.

Seven Rules for Encouraging Healthy Eating

1. Responsibility

A parent's *responsibility* is to provide nutritious food and regular mealtimes and snack times. The child's responsibility is to decide how much to eat. This is the golden rule for feeding children according to Ellyn Satter, a well-known nutritionist and author. Don't feel you have to determine how much your child eats, that is up to your child.

- Let your child make choices from a variety of good foods that you provide.
- Allow your child to determine how much to eat to satisfy hunger. Skipping a meal occasionally won't hurt a child. We all have times when we are less hungry.
- Learn to recognize when your baby doesn't want more food. Even infants know when they have had enough. They will turn their heads, push the spoon or food away, or protest verbally.
- Decide where your child should eat. Give food only at the table and don't allow running around while eating.
- Avoid coaxing, bribing, playing games, or force-feeding.

2. Respect

Respect a child's need to be cautious about trying new foods.

- Think about how you react to new foods. Do you dig right in or do you smell the food and take a tiny taste first? Children have less experience with food and may not be able to tell by the appearance or the smell whether they are likely to enjoy it. They may need to touch a new food and taste a bite and then remove it from their mouths.

- Encourage, but never force a child to try something new. Studies have shown that young children may need to try a new food **ten** times or more before accepting it. If a new food is rejected, offer it again at a later time.
- Remember that children are often sensitive to strong flavors. Broccoli, for example, may taste bitter to them. Don't worry, most adults like foods that they hated as kids.

3. Resist

Try to *resist* power struggles.

- Don't make mealtimes a battle. Choosing to eat is your child's job. Your job is to provide healthy food and to keep the atmosphere pleasant and relaxed.
- Don't try to force a child to eat. That is a battle you can't win. Refusing food can be a toddler's declaration of independence. Children who are pressured to eat actually end up eating less than those who are allowed to decide how much they want.
- Lighten up. Try what one dad does. When his preschooler complains about what is being served, he says, "Great, there will be more for me!" and calmly starts eating. This eliminates the power struggle and his daughter usually eats without a fuss.
- Give your child a choice between two equally healthy alternatives. For example, "Do you want an apple or a pear for a snack?" Involving children in the decision helps eliminate power struggles because they feel they have some control.
- Don't get into a struggle about how many bites of something your child needs to take. Meals can become a *bite count* and be very frustrating for everyone.

4. Replace

Gradually *replace* fluids with solid foods

- Limit juice to no more than 2–4 ounces a day for an infant, 4–6 ounces a day for a toddler. Put juice in a cup, not a bottle.
- Don't allow a child to carry around a bottle or cup of milk, juice, or soda. This practice reinforces eating for comfort, not just for hunger.
- Don't put your child to bed with a bottle.
- Encourage the use of a cup instead of a bottle at mealtimes as your child approaches one year of age. Offer solid foods first, then fluids.
- Wean your baby from the bottle by 12 to 15 months of age.
- Be aware that breast milk is not a nutritionally complete food for a toddler. If your child is not eating solids adequately, you may want to offer food first and offer the breast after the solids.

5. Reinforce

Reinforce good eating habits

- Remember that you know more about nutrition than your child does and you need to be in charge of what to serve. Don't give in to whining for junk food, but do allow your child to have an occasional treat.
- Don't use food as a way to keep a child entertained or quiet, provide toys instead.
- Establish regular meal times and snack times rather than allowing constant snacking or grazing.
- Don't give preschoolers caffeine and limit carbonated beverages and other junk food.
- Don't start cereals that are full of sugar and food coloring. Use them only as an occasional treat as you would candy. Don't offer to put sugar on unsweetened cereal.

- Encourage children to feed themselves when possible.
- Don't allow excessive playing with food. Give your child a warning and if the behavior persists remove the food and allow the child to get down from the table.
- Set a good example by eating and enjoying a variety of foods. Your little one learns by watching you.

6. Recognize

Learn to *recognize* correct portion sizes.

- Serving sizes for young children are very small. A serving is roughly one tablespoon per year of age.
- A large amount of food can be overwhelming to a child. Start small and offer more if your child finishes his first serving.
- The average child's growth is slower during the second year of life. A child this age may need smaller amounts of food because of this slowdown.

7. RELAX!

If you provide healthy foods, reasonably structured times for meals and snacks, and a nurturing atmosphere, you can trust your child to do the rest!

Solutions for Common Eating Behavior Problems

Still have questions about your child's eating behavior? Here are answers to some of the concerns parents often have about how to handle children's difficult eating behaviors:

What if my child wants only *junk foods* such as candy, chips, and soft drinks?

It is amazing how early kids gravitate to junk food! Children often learn to associate those foods with special times and consider them fun foods. Some children (and adults) prefer salty and sugary flavors. Also the heavy advertising of less healthy foods on television may influence a child to want them. Here's what you can do.

- Don't buy junk foods on a regular basis. It is easier to turn down requests for these foods if you don't have them in the house.
- Keep junk foods out of sight. If your child requests them you can say that those are foods you eat only once in a while and you are not serving them today, but you will have them again soon. Young children don't have a very clear sense of time, so you can be vague!
- Avoid characterizing any food as *forbidden* or *bad* because that makes it seem even more appealing. An occasional fast food meal or hot dog is not going to be a problem if most of what a child eats is nutritious. Some families have a relaxed meal once a week when pop and other junk food is allowed. Some prefer to have those foods less often.
- Teach children as young as three or four years of age about the effect of food on the body. You can explain that some of the foods that taste good are fine to have once in awhile, but that these foods don't provide everything our bodies need to be healthy. You can say, "Your body needs foods that help you grow."

- Encourage children to eat healthy foods by calling them growing, going, and glowing foods.
- Print out a copy of the food pyramid from the USDA website and help your child make choices of healthy foods from it. See our resource section.

What can I do if my child doesn't want foods touching on the plate?

- You can accommodate this preference by using a compartmentalized dish if you want. Many dishes made for young children are designed that way.
- If the food happens to touch and your child throws a tantrum, treat it as you would any other tantrum. Children who have tantrums at the table should be taken away from the table for a time-out. When they decide to finish eating without a fuss, they can be allowed to return to the table.

Why won't my child try new foods?

Food manufacturers are missing a great opportunity. If they could only make healthy foods look like chalk and crayons! Many finicky toddlers will munch on these but won't touch a new food.

There are several reasons that children this age are reluctant to try new foods. Young children like routines. They may insist on hearing the same bedtime story or wearing the same clothes every day. Preferring to eat the same food every day may be part of this developmental stage.

Preschoolers are also trying to decide what the rules are and are beginning to want some independence. Whenever you can, keep mealtimes pleasant and try to avoid power struggles. However, don't give into whining for snack foods or sweets, and don't become a *short-order cook*. Children learn to eat a variety of foods by being exposed to a variety of foods.

- Always have something on the table that your child will eat, such as fruit, milk, and whole-grain bread. If your child does not want the food you have prepared for the family, offer only the fruit and bread as alternatives.

- Encourage children to taste the new food, but do not coerce or pressure them to eat.
- Let your child see you enjoying the new food. Your child will eventually copy many of your food habits, likes, and dislikes.
- Don't give up. Keep offering foods that were previously rejected. Remember that children may need to be exposed to a food eight to ten times or more before they will eat it.
- Try having a one *bite rule.* Children can sometimes be convinced to try one bite of a food if they are allowed to take it out of their mouths if they don't like it.
- Let children participate in meal planning. They can be allowed to choose the main course for a meal once in awhile.
- Take children grocery shopping and allow them to choose a fruit or a vegetable to try.
- Invite preschoolers to help with food preparation. They may be willing to taste something that they help to prepare.
- Try **not** offering your child a new food. Enjoy it yourself and see if your child will be curious enough to ask for some.

How do I respond when my child just picks at dinner?

Remember the Responsibility Rule: A parent's responsibility is to provide nutritious food; the child's responsibility is to eat the correct quantity.

- Your child is the only one who knows how full or empty that little tummy is. Teach children to trust their appetites to determine how much they need. Don't try to force children to eat when they are not hungry. You can say, "Before you leave the table make sure your tummy is full."
- Children who whine about the food need to leave the table and return only if they decide to eat. Don't get angry, just calmly say, "You must not

be very hungry now. You can leave the table now." If your child decides to eat later, some of what was served for dinner can be warmed up.

- Children are often hungriest early in the day. If that is true for your child, try to give nutrition-packed breakfast foods. You can even offer the left-overs from your dinner the night before.

- When you have a big lunch you probably don't want much dinner that night. Young children often eat most of their calories early in the day and are just not hungry by evening. Since that may be the only meal the family eats together, parents of a child who has lunch at daycare may worry that their child is not eating enough because they don't see what has been eaten all day. If you are concerned, ask daycare providers to report what your child eats for lunch.

- The timing of the evening meal may be the problem. Children are often hungry and ready to eat dinner in the late afternoon and may be getting tired by the time you are ready to have dinner. Children who are tired may not have the patience to sit at the dinner table very long. If this seems to be a problem in your family, maybe it would be a good idea to have an earlier dinnertime for your little one. Your child can then join you at the table for the sociability and a snack while the adults have dinner.

I feel like a short-order cook!

All of us have favorite foods, but we don't expect to eat only those foods every day. Preschoolers often insist on having the same food every day. Your child needs to learn to eat a variety of foods. This variety is important for health and for social development. There is nothing worse than a teenager whose whims have been catered to and who will eat only one or two foods.

If your child wants the same food every day for lunch or snack that is probably okay as long as it is a reasonably healthy food. For example, a peanut butter sandwich and apple slices. However, when you are cooking for the entire family don't allow your child to have an entirely different meal. Offer what you are giving the family and always have something on the table that you know your child will eat, like bread and fruit. Encourage, but don't force your child to try the other food you are serving.

Prevention is always preferable to dealing with a firmly established habit. If your child is beginning to insist on only macaroni and cheese, for example, nip that idea in the bud. Some ideas for preventing this problem:

As the parent, you should be the one to decide what to serve for meals and snacks.

- Explain that you aren't serving that food today, but will have it again soon. Some children will be satisfied with this explanation. For children who respond with a tantrum, explain kindly but firmly that no one has to eat unless they want to.
- Eat your food and let your child decide what to do. Chances are your child will decide to sit down and join the rest of the family for the meal.

What if it is too late for prevention? You have already given in and fixed macaroni and cheese every night for the past six months because you want your child to eat something. The sooner you change the better. Here is something you can try with a child who is about three or older:

- Get a colorful calendar and sit down with your child and the calendar.
- Explain that our bodies need a variety of foods. There are a lot of foods that taste good and are good for us.
- Tell your child that every Monday (or whatever day you choose) you will make macaroni and cheese. The other days you will not be making it but will fix other things that are good to eat.
- Put the calendar up where your child can see it and put a sticker on the day of the week each morning. Put a special mark on the day you are having macaroni and cheese. Your preschooler will also learn about calendars as part of this project.
- Make sure that all adults involved with feeding the child—parents, grandparents, nanny, etc., will commit to the program.

- Allow your child to decide whether to eat and how much to eat. Children need to sit at the table with the family for at least a short time, but they don't have to eat. If your child whines about not having the favorite food, don't give in.

Your approach to this project is very important. Keep a friendly matter-of-fact manner. Don't coerce, cajole, or bribe your child to eat what you are offering. The less you say about it the better. Just assume that your child will eat with the rest of the family.

You may be surprised how soon your child will decide to try some of what you are eating.

My toddler is dependent on the bottle—what should I do?

Most infants are ready to start weaning from the bottle at about 10 to 12 months of age and should be completely weaned by 12 to 15 months of age. Continuing beyond that age can result in a poor appetite because too many calories are being taken in fluid form. If a child is breastfeeding, it is a good idea to offer the solids foods first and the breast second at mealtimes. While breast milk is good for infants and can be beneficial for toddlers as well, it doesn't contain all the nutrition that toddlers need. They need to have a variety of foods to meet their nutritional needs and to develop eating skills. Try these techniques to help reduce your toddler's dependence on the bottle:

- Initially, restrict the bottle to mealtimes and offer it only after the solid foods have been eaten.
- Next, for at least one meal a day put milk in a cup instead of a bottle.
- Don't allow a toddler to carry around a bottle of milk, juice, or soda.
- Serve juice only in a cup, not a bottle.
- Don't replace bottle nipples and pacifiers as they wear out.
- Try to find a bedtime routine such as reading a book or singing and snuggling rather than depending on the bottle to lull a child to sleep.

- Don't *ever* put a child to bed with a bottle. Falling asleep with the bottle can cause dental cavities.

- Try weaning children older than two *cold turkey*. Plan a *growing up party* with your child. Buy a special new cup to drink from. Invite a friend or two to come celebrate or just have a party with the family. Your child can help pack up the bottles and pacifiers and put them away if you plan to use them for a future baby. If you won't need the bottles again, box them up and drop them off at a thrift store. (Don't donate pacifiers.)

How can I stop my child from playing with food?

When children are beginning to eat by themselves, they use their fingers to pick up their food. They may also touch or poke at a new food to find out about it. This is part of learning about food and can be allowed up to a point. Just protect the floor so the cleanup is easier. However, children shouldn't be allowed to just play with food or to throw food on the floor.

- Allow your child to help you prepare food. That will provide a good opportunity to experiment with the *feel* of food.

- Let children know that they need to leave the table if they are just playing with their food.

- Try some of the recipes for playdough and other hands-on activities in our **Food for Play** chapter to give your child tactile experiences.

What if my child won't eat the green stuff?

Some children's theme song should be "It's not *easy eating* green!" This dislike is not at all unusual for young children. They often have a preference for sweet flavors and have to develop a taste for vegetables. Sometimes the harder you try, the more they resist. Here are some hints:

- Don't make too big an issue of the vegetables for now. Keep offering them and letting your child see you eat a variety of vegetables.

- Try what one mother we know did. She said vegetables are *grown up food*. She let her child see her enjoying vegetables but didn't offer them. It wasn't long until her child was begging to be allowed to try the forbidden food.
- Try adding vegetables to soups, muffins, breads, cookies, pancakes, sandwiches, casseroles, spaghetti sauce, meat loaf, etc. Grate, chop, or purée them if necessary to hide them. For example, grated carrots can be added to tuna for sandwich filling.
- Serve cooked vegetables with cheese sauce, butter, or even catsup. Try raw or steamed vegetables with dips.
- Try Asian-style stir-fried vegetables.
- Don't give up—keep offering vegetables and your child will develop a taste for some of them.
- Offer fruits, especially the dark colored fruits such as cantaloupe, nectarines, peaches, plums, apricots, and berries. They provide similar nutrition.
- Try the *one-bite rule*. Encourage your child to take one bite to taste the food.

What should I do if my child will drink only juice and not milk?

- Limit your child to a maximum of four to six ounces of juice a day. Juice provides some vitamins but does not have the vitamin D or protein a child needs. Juice also has a lot of calories, so it is easy for a child to fill up on juice, taking away the appetite for other foods.
- Let your child know that juice will be served only once a day. Don't give into tantrums or whining for more. Offer water or milk as alternatives the rest of the day.
- If a child continues to refuse milk, offer yogurt, cheese, chocolate milk, cottage cheese, milk-based soups, and puddings.

- Cheese and yogurt generally don't contain vitamin D. If these are the only dairy products your child will take, give a daily multivitamin.
- Try making fruit drinks that contain milk or yogurt. Look in our Beverage chapter for some great ideas.
- Offer milk as a beverage with every meal.
- Try offering milk at room temperature or with a straw.
- Use milk instead of water when cooking cereal or soups. Add it to casseroles, meat loafs, etc.
- Use cheese in cooking.
- Try putting some powdered milk into the batter when you bake muffins, pancakes, waffles, or cookies. You can add two tablespoons of powdered milk per cup of flour in recipes for baked products.
- Try vitamin D and calcium-enriched soy or rice milk if your child doesn't like the flavor of milk.
- Ask your doctor about a vitamin D and calcium supplement if your child refuses all dairy products.

How about if my child wants to eat on the run?

Once children can walk and run, they want to be on the go, exploring and moving. Getting them to sit still for anything can be challenging. They depend on adults to set limits to their behavior—when eating as well as other times.

- Children need to sit at the table or in a high chair for meals and snacks. Eating while running around is dangerous because it can cause choking. In fact, most choking occurs when children are running with food in their mouths.
- Children, and adults, are more likely to eat nutritious food if snacks are planned for and eaten while sitting at the table.

- Active children may be unable to stay at the table for the whole meal. When they have finished eating, it's fine to allow them to leave the table. If they come back for more, don't give handouts. Make sitting at the table a requirement for eating.

What do I do if my child won't swallow the food?

Sometimes toddlers will hold food in their cheeks rather than swallowing it. If this is happening, make sure you are not putting too much pressure on your child to eat. Children may put food into their mouths to satisfy a parent's demands, but may not want to swallow the food. Running around with *pouched* food in the mouth is a choking hazard. If your child is under two, you may be able to remove the food with your finger. Older children can be told they need to either swallow the food or take it out of their mouths before getting down from the table. Try to make sure that they don't try to swallow too much at one time.

How can I discourage my child from sneaking food?

Usually children sneak food because there is something they feel they are not being allowed to eat as often as they would like.

- Make sure the food is available to them at appropriate times. This can sometimes solve the problem. For example, if they always sneak peanut butter, let them have as much as they want every day at lunch or snack time. Perhaps if they know they can have all they want at a particular time, they won't feel the need to get into the food at other times.
- Be aware that preschoolers can be pretty impulsive. Seeing a favorite food may make them think they want some and they may impulsively get into it. Even adults will eat impulsively if they see a food they like. You may have to keep the food a child sneaks out of sight and out of reach.
- You may have to stop buying *junk foods* for now if your child is sneaking them.

- Make sure your child is not getting excessively hungry between meals. Most preschool children need to eat at least every three hours. Offer meals and snacks on a regular basis.
- Be sure that children are getting their emotional needs met with time and attention from parents. Sometimes sneaking food is a way to try to satisfy other needs.

I am worried that my child is underweight.

Being light in weight is not necessarily bad. For children with a small bone structure who are otherwise healthy and eating well, it may be normal to be small.

- Consult your doctor if your child has chronic diarrhea, abdominal pain, or is frequently ill.
- Look at body types and growth patterns in the extended family. Are there other people who are slim but healthy? Or are there people who were petite and slim as children who bulked up as they matured?

My child won't drink water—should I worry about that?

Water is important for people of all ages. It's essential for kidney function and helps to prevent dehydration and constipation. Children need to drink enough water to quench their thirst, depending upon the weather, activity level, and body size. More is needed in hot weather or when sweating. If your child's urine is dark yellow or has a strong odor that may indicate a need for more water. You might try some of these ideas to encourage your little one to drink more water:

- Try to make sure you drink enough water and offer your child water every time you get a drink.
- Offer water with between meal snacks.

- Offer preschoolers water often. They may not ask for a drink of water when they are busy playing.
- Ask that daycare and preschool caregivers encourage the children to drink water.
- Try giving your child a special straw, cup, or sports bottle.
- Carry a water bottle with you when you run errands.
- Keep a pitcher of water in the refrigerator.
- Add a little fresh lemon or lime to water occasionally to flavor it.
- Always have water on the table at mealtimes in addition to milk.
- Offer soups and other liquid foods.

Preventing Eating Disorders

Eating disorders are unhealthy patterns of behavior that can be associated with serious health consequences. All eating disorders, whether anorexia, bulimia, or binge eating, involve abnormalities in body image and loss of control of eating. They occur most often in adolescent girls and adult women, but can affect boys and men as well. Unfortunately, our society admires thinness. Only a small percentage of people are genetically programmed to have the body-type that is currently considered most attractive. The rest have to chronically undereat to achieve this unhealthy goal. Children and adults need to realize that a strong, healthy body is what matters, not a certain number of pounds on the scale.

Why include this topic in a book about feeding young children? Attitudes about eating begin very early in life. Parents have an opportunity to help their child develop healthy attitudes about food and eating. Learning to trust their appetites and to eat a healthy variety of foods gives children a good chance of avoiding later eating disorders.

Body Image

- Never criticize your child's physical appearance.
- Teach your child to appreciate people for qualities other than appearance.
- Encourage active play and the development of physical skills.
- Give children dolls that represent normal body types—consider avoiding the fashion dolls that have completely unrealistic body proportions.
- Don't point out or criticize people who are overweight.
- Try not to overemphasize physical beauty. Stress good health and strength.
- Accept the body type that is healthy for your child. Try not to have unrealistic expectations. Healthy children and adults come in a variety of shapes and sizes.
- Avoid criticizing your body around your child.

Recognizing Body Signals of Hunger and Satiety

- Trust your child's appetite. Don't press children to eat when they are ready to stop. Even infants can determine when they have had enough.
- Don't press children to continue eating if they do not want to. Unlike most adults, children are naturally sensitive to appetite and will stop in the middle of eating a favorite food if they get full. This responsiveness is something to encourage.
- Feed your child for hunger and not comfort. When your child is distressed, offer hugs instead of food.

- Don't use food to relieve boredom.
- Try to avoid using food as a way to keep a child entertained or quiet.
- Drop out of the *clean plate club*.
- Encourage children who are old enough to serve themselves.

Attitudes about Food

- Establish regular meal times and snack times and don't permit constant snacking.
- Don't restrict healthy food. Allow your child to eat as much as needed to feel satisfied at meal and snack times.
- Seek treatment if you have an eating disorder. If you cannot come to terms with your relationship with food, it will be hard to help your child develop a healthy attitude about food.
- Set a good example by eating and enjoying healthy food.
- Don't use food as a reward. Try to use special activities, praise, and time with parents instead.
- Try to have a balanced approach to eating. Don't totally prohibit an occasional treat.

Attitudes about Physical Activity

- Don't talk about exercise as a chore. Instead, find a way to be active just for the enjoyment of it.
- Encourage your young child to learn to enjoy jumping, running, climbing, and other physical activities.
- Set a good example by being physically active yourself, not just a spectator for your children's activities.

- Don't avoid physical activities such as swimming because you feel you are overweight.

Understanding and Preventing Obesity

Obesity is a frequent nutritional disease of children in the United States and other developed countries. The incidence of childhood obesity has increased dramatically in the last twenty years. Many experts believe that one child in three is either overweight or at risk of becoming overweight. Children who are overweight at age three and older are twice as likely to be obese as adults than are children with normal weights. Chronically overweight children are vulnerable to social problems, poor self-esteem, high cholesterol levels, diabetes, and later heart disease. Since healthy eating habits can be established during the preschool years, you have a great opportunity to get your child off to a good start.

Causes of Obesity in Children

Obesity is caused by a combination of genetic and environmental factors. Some have estimated that it is 5–25% genetics, and 75–95% environment. The genetic influence cannot be changed, but the environmental influence can be modified. A major environmental factor is inactivity, due to too much time spent watching television and snacking rather than participating in active play. Dietary factors such as excessive fat intake and inadequate fiber intake are also causes.

Parental overcontrol of eating has also been shown to be related to obesity. Many of the guidelines for preventing eating disorders apply to preventing obesity. Children whose eating is overcontrolled fail to learn to recognize their internal hunger and satiety signals. Children must learn to self-regulate their eating. Pressing children to eat when they are not hungry can lead either to overeating or to finicky eating.

How to Tell if Your Child is Overweight

The first step is to have accurate height and weight measurements. The measurements can then be plotted on a standardized growth chart to determine how your child compares with other children of the same age. The growth charts produced by the Center for Disease Control and released in May of 2000 include, for the first time, a body mass index-for-age chart for children over age two. Body mass index or BMI is a number calculated from weight and height measurements to determine if weight is appropriate for height.

Directions for calculating your child's body mass index are in the Growth Chart Section of this book. If a child's body mass index is 95th percentile or higher the child is considered overweight. Between the 85th percentile and 95th percentile a child is considered at risk for becoming overweight.

What to Do if Your Child is Overweight

If you have a serious concern about your child's weight, get advice from your pediatrician or a pediatric nutrition specialist. Minor changes in diet and activity level may help. Because children are growing, small changes can have significant long-term effects. If your child prefers sedentary activities substituting physical activity for television and computer time is a good place to start. Children who watch one hour or less of television per day are measurably leaner than those who spend more time in front of the tube.

It is very important not to become too controlling about your child's eating. A coercive approach will backfire in the long run. Children whose eating is over-controlled may feel deprived and unloved. Also growing children need a lot of calories and cannot diet the way adults can. The goal is to help develop the body shape that is most healthy for your child. Children need to learn to respond to their body hunger signals by eating healthy foods. Above all, don't criticize your child's appearance, but accept your child's natural body type. Children need to know that their parents love them unconditionally.

An Ounce of Prevention May Equal a Pound of Cure

Follow these principles to help prevent your child from developing obesity.

First year of life

- Help your baby learn to use human contact for comfort rather than food. An infant's crying may not mean hunger. Babies also cry if they are bored or need some other kind of attention.
- Breastfeed if possible, as breastfed babies tend to be lighter in weight.
- Respect your baby's appetite. Don't try to insist that every bottle is finished.
- Don't start solids until after 4 months of age.
- Don't overfeed babies. Spoon-fed infants will turn their heads or close their mouths when they are finished eating.
- Don't put your baby or toddler to bed with a bottle. That teaches your child to eat frequently and to use food for comfort.
- Don't over-react if your baby is chubby; check your family history. In some families, infants are chubby but end up as adults with healthy weights.

Age one to two years

- Start weaning from the breast or bottle at 10 to 12 months of age and complete bottle weaning by 15 months. Delayed weaning from the bottle is associated with obesity. If you want to continue breastfeeding beyond that time, be sure your child is eating a variety of healthy solids.
- Don't use food to keep a child entertained. Keep a box of toys that you bring out for your child to play with when you need to get something done.
- Don't allow a toddler to carry a cup or bottle of juice, milk, or soda to drink from constantly.
- Limit juice intake to 4 ounces a day. Encourage water to quench thirst.

- Start with unsugared cereals and whole grain bread and cereal products from the beginning.
- Don't require your child to eat everything on the plate. Let your child's appetite be the guide to how much is eaten.
- Don't give carbonated drinks or candy to children this age.age two.

Age two to five years

- Offer lowfat or nonfat dairy products.
- Limit juice to 6 ounces a day. Give your child water to quench thirst.
- Offer fruits and vegetables as snacks.
- Avoid carbonated drinks and candy except for special occasions.
- Don't purchase *junk food* on a regular basis.
- Limit trips to fast food restaurants.
- Try to avoid the TV-food connection. Don't eat meals or snacks in front of the television, except on special occasions.
- Have two or three between-meal snack times rather than constantly grazing.
- Don't completely forbid sweets and treats as that may make them more attractive.
- Encourage children to trust their appetites. Don't press them to eat if they don't want to.
- Serve fresh fruits for dessert.
- Reserve sugared cereals for special times such as birthdays or holidays.
- Give your child the choice of healthy foods, for example an apple or a pear, not an apple or potato chips.
- Let your child choose a new vegetable or fruit to try.

- Use praise, hugs, special activities, stickers, or time with a parent as rewards rather than food. Use food rewards only for special situations such as problems with toilet training.

Fitness Activities

- Encourage at least 30 minutes of physical activity a day.
- Set a good example. Children of active parents are six times more likely to be active. By improving your fitness you also help your child!
- Exercise to lively music or a video and your preschooler will want to join you.
- Let your child help you garden. Children love playing in dirt. You won't get as much done, but maybe it will pay off when your little one becomes a teenager!
- Limit television watching and playing computer games to a maximum of one or two hours a day.
- Provide play equipment such as tricycles, wagons, pull toys, large rubber balls, doll carriages, and climbing toys.
- Play with your child. For example play tag, ball or hide-and-seek.
- Make regular visits to parks or indoor play areas.
- Don't carry a child who is able to walk.
- Encourage outdoor play. Children enjoy playing outside or taking walks in all kinds of weather. Just make sure they are dressed appropriately.
- Don't overuse the stroller. Encourage your child to walk whenever it is safe.
- Walk instead of driving when possible.
- Consider enrolling your child in gymnastics, swimming, or dancing lessons.
- Make sure your child's preschool or daycare encourages active play.

Table-Time Tips for Family Meals

Family meals are important social times. Children can learn manners, good eating habits, and conversational skills by sharing meals with other family members.

- Turn off the television at mealtime.
- Sit with your child at the table to encourage socializing at mealtimes.
- Ignore tantrums. If children persist with whining or tantrums, they need to leave the table until they are ready to behave.
- Don't allow endless complaints about the food. Even young children can begin to learn to say, "no thanks," or, "yes please," when offered a food.
- Expect messes when young children are learning to feed themselves. Be patient and be prepared by protecting the floor and having a cloth nearby to wipe up spills.
- Babies who are able to sit in a high chair without help, should join the family for at least part of a meal even if they are not eating much solid food. This helps them socialize with the family and learn eating behaviors.
- Provide safe, comfortable seating for young children including support for their feet.
- Involve children in food preparation and table setting and clearing when possible.
- Use child-sized eating utensils, plates, and cups to make mealtimes easier.
- Don't always cater to your child's tastes. Family meals are a great time to introduce your child to the foods you enjoy.
- Remember to let your child decide how much to eat and you will avoid a lot of mealtime conflicts.
- Let your child leave the table when finished eating.

Eating Out with Preschoolers

Families are eating more of their meals in restaurants than ever before. Here are some tips to make your eating-out experiences more enjoyable.

Signs of a Tot-Friendly Restaurant

- Caters to children: has fast service, safe high chairs, and food that children like.
- Offers a children's menu with portions that are smaller than those for adults.
- Has a salad or pasta bar so food is available immediately.
- Is not too crowded at the time you want to eat.
- Has a relaxed environment; avoid formal restaurants that are more suited for adults.

What to Take with You

- Diaper wipes or hand sanitizer.
- Snacks such as crackers or cheese cubes.
- Extra diapers and a change of clothes.
- A bib, spoon, plastic dish, tippy cup, or bottle.
- A few simple toys.
- Crayons or washable markers for drawing on paper placemats.

Safety Tips

- Ask that undercooked meat, poultry, or egg dishes be redone.
- Avoid unpasteurized juices, ciders, milk, or cheese.

- Taste your child's food. A young child may not recognize that something is spoiled.
- Refuse hard candies or other foods that are choking hazards.
- Move breakable dishes, sharp utensils, hot dishes, and hot beverages out of reach.
- Be sure the high chair or booster chair has a safety strap and cannot tip over.
- Don't sit in a high traffic area where waiters or others could spill food or bump into your child.
- Ask to be seated in the nonsmoking section

What to Order:

- Pasta, mashed potatoes, or steamed vegetables.
- An appetizer or something else (such as a fruit plate) that can be brought right away.
- Child-sized portions or side dishes.
- Special order with less seasoning if the dish might be spicy.
- Special order if there is not a good choice on the menu and consider leaving a bigger tip for the server and cook.
- A cup with a lid if available.
- Extra napkins so you are ready to clean up spills.

Encouraging Good Behavior:

- Be realistic about how long your child can sit still and behave.
- Go out for breakfast or lunch instead of dinner. The meal will cost less and your child may be better behaved early in the day.
- Don't go out to eat when it is your child's naptime.
- Call in an order ahead of time so there is no wait for the food.
- After ordering, one parent can take the child outside until the meal is ready.
- Before leaving home, tell your child what kind of behavior you expect.
- If your child finishes eating before you do, offer toys, crayons or other activities to keep your little one occupied while you eat.
- Try to sit near a window or a fish tank.
- Practice at home. Let your child dress up and practice good restaurant behavior. Children also enjoy taking a turn at playing the waiter.
- Be considerate of the other guests. If your child misbehaves and can't be calmed by a time out, ask for a doggy bag for the uneaten food and finish your meal at home.

Chapter 13

Food and Health

Food allergies, food safety, and feeding sick kids

You have probably received lots of well-meaning advice about how and what to feed your child:

"Don't give children milk if they have colds—it makes mucous."

"Babies who have rashes must be allergic to something they are eating."

"If your baby has colic it must be from your milk."

"Don't let your baby eat that—it will cause choking."

If all of this advice has left you confused, this chapter is just what you need. It will provide you with the basics about what to feed a sick child, how to recognize food allergies, steps to prevent food poisoning, how to prevent choking, and how to keep your child safe in the kitchen.

Food and Health

What to Feed Them When They're Sick

Upper Respiratory Infections

Fever

Gastroenteritis

- *Vomiting*
- *Diarrhea*

Constipation

Colic

Food Allergies

Symptoms of Food Allergy

Common Allergenic Foods

Treatment

Prevention

Food Poisoning

Food Safety Quiz

Food Poisoning Prevention Tips

Drinking Water Safety Guidelines

Choking

Common Causes

Preventive Measures

Kitchen Safety

What to Feed Them When They're Sick

Is it *feed a cold* and *starve a fever* or vice versa? When your child is sick you're stressed enough without having to worry about what food is best. It can be hard to find things that healthy toddlers will eat. When they're sick, it's even worse. Sick children may have smaller appetites than usual, causing parents to worry that their child won't get enough nutrition. This brief guide addresses concerns about feeding young children when they're sick.

Upper Respiratory Infections

Upper respiratory infections include colds, coughs, and croup. When your child has an upper respiratory infection extra fluids are required to keep the mucous secretions from getting too thick. A child may also lose fluid by coughing, having a runny nose, and running a fever. A stuffy nose may affect the ability to smell food, resulting in a reduced appetite. A sore throat may make swallowing uncomfortable. What's a parent to do?

Here are some tips:

- When infants have stuffy noses, they often have trouble nursing or feeding from a bottle. Putting a few drops of saline in the nose then suctioning with a bulb syringe may help. Saline drops may be purchased at the drug store.
- It is fine to allow a child with a cough or a cold to have milk. It does not cause the production of mucous.
- Warm liquids such as soups and hot chocolate may be comforting to a child with a stuffy nose and cough and may make breathing more comfortable.
- Soft foods and cold liquids may feel best to a child with a sore throat. Try yogurt, applesauce, finger gelatin, pudding, ice cream, frozen fruit bars and canned fruits.
- Don't worry too much if your child eats less for a few days as long as enough fluids are taken to maintain urine output. When children are sick they are usually less active. They don't need as many calories as when they are well.

- Offer familiar and favorite foods when your child is sick. This is not a good time to try something new.
- The jury is still out about the value of extra vitamin C. We don't recommend giving supplements, but you can encourage vitamin rich fruit and fruit juices.
- Don't give your young child herbal remedies. They are not proven to be safe for children.
- Consult your doctor before giving infants and toddlers over-the-counter remedies.

Call the doctor if your child:

- Is less than one year of age
- Is lethargic
- Can't sleep at night
- Complains of ear pain or chest pain
- Has difficulty breathing
- Is not improving after 7-10 days
- Has a cough accompanied by a fever

Follow your intuition and call your doctor if you are worried

Fever

Fevers cause loss of fluids through sweating and loss of calories through increased metabolic rate. Since appetite may also be reduced, children who have fevers for a few days may lose weight. However, they will generally eat more than usual when they recover and will quickly regain the lost weight.

Here are some hints for feeding a feverish child:

- Children who are not taking fluids well are often willing to eat popsicles as a source of liquid. Regular popsicles are just sweetened and colored frozen water. Offer frozen juice bars for more nutrition.
- If your child has a small appetite, concentrate on fluids. Don't worry too much about intake of solid foods while a child is feverish
- Cold foods may be appealing and may help reduce the fever.
- Try mild foods such as yogurt, applesauce, pudding, ice cream, fruit smoothies and finger gelatins.
- If the temperature is over 101°F, giving acetaminophen (Tylenol, for example) or ibuprofen (Motrin or Advil, for example) to reduce fever may help a child feel more like eating.

Call the doctor if your child:

- Is less than one year of age
- Is lethargic or confused
- Has a headache or stiff neck
- Refuses to take fluids
- Has a fever and a rash

Follow your intuition and call your doctor if you are worried

Gastroenteritis (Stomach Flu)

Gastroenteritis, or stomach flu, is common in young children. Symptoms may include abdominal cramping, vomiting, and diarrhea.

Vomiting

- If an infant cannot keep down breast milk or formula, offer commercial replacement fluids such as Pedialyte or KaoLectrolyte to replace important minerals. Water, diluted juice, or overly diluted formula can cause water intoxication. This serious imbalance of blood minerals may cause seizures and can even be fatal.
- After your child vomits, wait an hour before offering anything else to eat or drink. This will allow the stomach to calm down so vomiting again is less likely.
- After an hour, give no more than an ounce of a clear liquid and wait fifteen minutes to see if it stays down. If it does, offer an ounce every fifteen minutes for an hour. If there is no more vomiting, gradually increase the amount of fluid offered.
- If vomiting is repeated, wait for another half-hour and try offering sips of clear liquids. If that stays down, offer sips every fifteen minutes. Gradually increase the amount offered.
- Clear liquids such as Pedialyte, KaoLectrolyte, white grape juice, flat ginger ale, 7-Up, and Sprite often stay down better than water. They also have the advantage of supplying some calories.
- Don't make homemade salt or soda solutions to give to vomiting children. They can be dangerous if they don't provide exactly the right amount of minerals.
- Don't give diet sodas, diet popsicles, or sugar-free gelatins which contain no calories.
- If your child refuses to drink, try serving clear liquids frozen as popsicles.
- Encourage, but don't force, your child to drink. Forcing may cause more nausea and vomiting.
- Monitor your child's fluid intake and urine output and urine color. As children become dehydrated they urinate less and their urine is darker in color.

- When your child is consistently keeping down fluids, you can try offering some solids.
- The BRAT diet, which stands for Banana, Rice, Apple, and Toast, has been recommended in the past. You can follow the BRAT diet if you want to but it is not necessary to avoid other mild foods that your child enjoys. Examples might be yogurt, soda crackers, pretzels, dry toast, and clear soups.

Diarrhea

- If your child is not vomiting, encourage fluid intake to make up for the fluids lost in the stool. Your child can continue breast milk or cow's milk as usual. Offer commercial replacement fluids in addition.
- If your child has both vomiting and diarrhea, try the steps described under Vomiting.
- Monitor your child's urine output, urine color and activity level. A child who has both vomiting and diarrhea can easily become dehydrated.
- Yogurt containing a live culture may be beneficial when taking an antibiotic that causes diarrhea. Milk, however, may not be digested well due to temporary difficulty digesting lactose. Soy milk, lactose-free milk, or rice milk may be better tolerated.
- Don't restrict the amount of food your child eats. Allow enough food to satisfy appetite.
- Your child may eat mild foods. Just avoid high-fat and high-fiber foods. See the comments about the BRAT diet under Treatment for Vomiting.

Call the doctor if your child:

- Is less than one year old
- Is lethargic
- Has a fever

- Cannot keep down sips of fluid
- Vomits more than two or three times in a 24 hour period
- Vomits for more than one day
- Vomits bile or blood
- Has persistent or severe abdominal pain
- Has bloody diarrhea
- Has diarrhea for more than two days
- Has profuse watery stools
- Has decreased urine output, dark urine, sunken eyes, or dry mouth

Follow your intuition and call your doctor if you are worried

Constipation

Constipation is defined as infrequent, hard and sometimes painful stools. Insufficient fiber and fluids in the diet can cause constipation. It can also occur when a child is being toilet trained. Some children resist sitting on the toilet to have a stool and will hold back, causing their stools to be large and hard.

- Increase the high-fiber foods in your child's diet. Foods that are high in fiber include most fruits and vegetables, legumes, oatmeal, bran, brown rice, whole-grain breads, waffles, muffins, cereals, and crackers.
- Try some of the high-fiber recipes in this book.
- Choose prepared foods that list high-fiber products as the first ingredient.
- Offer your child water frequently.
- Prune juice, apple juice, and pear juice contain natural ingredients that have a laxative effect and can be helpful for treating constipation. Limit juice intake to 2–4 ounces a day for an infant, 4–6 ounces a day for children over one year of age.

- Fiber supplements, mineral oil, or laxatives are only recommended if a child has encopresis (stool holding and bowel accidents). Talk with your pediatrician before using these on a regular basis.
- If your child is toilet-trained, encourage sitting on the toilet to have a bowel movement at the same time every day. This can be especially effective right after breakfast when there is a natural tendency to produce a stool.

Call your doctor if:

- There is blood in your child's stool
- Constipation persists in spite of changing the diet
- You need advice about whether to use a laxative or other medication
- Bowel accidents are continuing in a toilet-trained child

Colic

Babies who cry excessively may have colic. Colic is inconsolable crying that occurs during the first few months of life. Usually the bouts of crying are in the afternoon or evening. When babies with colic cry, their abdominal muscles feel firm and they draw up their legs. This does not mean that they have tummy pain. The abdominal muscles feel hard because the muscles are being used for crying. Drawing up the legs is a normal crying posture. Colic usually is much better or even completely gone by the time the baby is three months of age. While we are not sure of the cause, babies with colic seem to have sensitive temperaments. Even when the colic ends they may continue to be intense and reactive.

Treatment for Colic:

Your baby's discomfort is probably not caused by anything in the diet, but here are some things you can try:

- Consult your pediatrician to be sure there is no other explanation for your baby's fussiness.

- If your baby also has vomiting, diarrhea, or eczema, you could try a formula change. Eliminate cow's milk formula and use soy formula instead. If this doesn't help, ask your doctor to recommend one of the hypoallergenic formulas.
- If you are breastfeeding, try reducing your caffeine intake.
- Occasionally cow's milk in mother's diet seems to be related to a breastfeeding baby's colic. Try eliminating cow's milk and milk products from your diet for a few days. If that seems helpful talk to your doctor about other sources of calcium and vitamin D.
- Don't use herbal remedies without checking with your pediatrician. Just because a product is natural and comes from a plant does not mean it is safe for babies.
- Since colic is not caused by intestinal gas, excessive efforts to burp your baby are not helpful. Simethicone drops to reduce gas are harmless, but probably won't help.
- Don't overfeed your baby. On the other hand, if you are breastfeeding, be sure your baby is taking enough milk. A breastfeeding baby should have wet diapers every three to four hours once mother's milk is in.
- Make sure your baby is not being over-stimulated. Some babies overreact to noise and jostling.
- Carrying your baby in a front pack as you go about your day may help. Also try rocking a crying baby in a cradle or rocking chair.
- Some babies will calm when they are in a wind-up swing or when they are taken for a ride in the car.
- If nothing helps, some babies can be calmed by being swaddled in a receiving blanket and placed on their backs in the crib or bassinet. Letting babies cry for 15 minutes or so may allow them to fall asleep. If they are still crying after 15 minutes, holding and rocking them may be soothing. Some babies seem to need to let off steam by crying before they can be calmed.

- Take a nap when your baby naps so you are better able to cope with the long nights.
- Caring for a colicky baby is exhausting. If you are feeling irritated with your baby, it is important to get some help. Ask for help from your spouse or a friend. If no one is available, consider hiring an experienced babysitter for an hour or two so you can get out of the house for a short time.

Food Allergies

Food allergies tend to be overdiagnosed. Only about 5% of children are truly allergic to a food. Allergic reactions are caused by an immune system reaction. Not all reactions to foods are caused by allergy. For example, lactose intolerance may cause diarrhea and gassiness after drinking milk or eating dairy products. Lactose intolerance is the lack of an intestinal enzyme that is necessary to digest the lactose (milk sugar) in milk. Another example of a food intolerance that is not allergy is celiac sprue, also called gluten enteropathy. People with sprue cannot tolerate gluten, which is found in wheat, oats, barley, and rye. Sprue is usually hereditary and is caused by a gastrointestinal tract abnormality.

Symptoms of food allergy

- Hives or other skin rashes
- Swelling of the lips or tongue
- Itchy palate
- Tight feeling in throat
- Vomiting, diarrhea
- Nasal congestion
- Wheezing or difficulty breathing
- Anaphylaxis—a sudden and severe life threatening reaction with wheezing, hives, swelling of the throat and shock

Common allergenic foods

Milk, eggs, peanuts, other nuts, wheat, soy, fish, and shellfish. The foods most likely to cause anaphylactic reactions are peanuts, other nuts, shellfish, and eggs. Peanuts are the most common cause of serious reactions.

Treatment

If you suspect that your child has had a reaction to a food consult with your physician or an allergist before giving that food again. Your child may need allergy tests. A pediatric allergist can do blood tests or skin tests to help determine whether your child is allergic. Sometimes a food challenge will be done under a doctor's supervision. If your child is proven to be allergic to an important food such as milk and has to avoid the food, it may be necessary to give vitamin and mineral supplements. Consult a pediatric registered dietitian for an evaluation of your child's diet. See the Appendix in the back of this book for web sites that provide good information.

Anaphylactic reactions to foods can be fatal! Anyone with this type of allergy **must** avoid the food and **must** have an emergency epinephrine injection on hand at all times. Even a tiny amount of the food they are allergic to can be extremely dangerous. More people die each year from anaphylaxis to foods than from reactions to stinging insects, so these reactions need to be taken seriously.

Prevention

It is impossible to totally prevent food allergies. However if you have a strong family history of food allergy, there are some things you could consider doing:

- Breastfeed for the first year of life or feed a hypoallergenic infant formula (consult with your pediatrician for a recommendation).
- Avoid eating milk products, peanuts, and eggs while you are breastfeeding. Infants can be sensitized to these foods through breast milk.

- Don't feed your infant any solid foods until after the age of 6 months.
- Avoid giving cow's milk products, egg whites, soy protein, fish, wheat, and citrus foods for the first 12 months.
- Avoid giving peanuts, peanut butter, other nuts, and shellfish before 3 or 4 years of age.

Food Poisoning

When is vomiting and diarrhea not *stomach flu?* When it's food poisoning. Food poisoning is more common than you might realize. Symptoms of food poisoning can be identical to those of gastroenteritis. Young children are particularly susceptible since their immune systems are immature. Protect your child from this serious problem. Test your food safety IQ with our Food Safety Quiz, then read the food poisoning prevention tips.

Food Safety Quiz

Classify the following statements as True or False.

1. Symptoms of food poisoning usually start within 24 hours of eating contaminated food.
2. Unpasteurized fruit juice can cause e. coli and salmonella poisoning.
3. Contaminated food usually looks, smells or tastes spoiled.
4. Hot leftover food should be cooled at room temperature before putting it away in the refrigerator.
5. Honey is a nutritious natural food for infants.
6. A cutting board should be thoroughly washed in hot soapy water after preparing raw meat or poultry.
7. Fruits and vegetables can carry dangerous bacteria.
8. Eggs can be safely stored in the shelf on the refrigerator door.

9. It is fine to keep colored hard-boiled Easter eggs at room temperature for up to 48 hours.
10. The best way to defrost meat is slowly at room temperature.
11. Ground beef kept in the freezer for 6 months is still safe to eat.
12. The only sure way to know whether meat is safely cooked is with a thermometer.
13. Most food poisoning results from eating at a fast food restaurant.
14. Food poisoning is actually not very common in the United States.
15. It is important to practice safe food-handling measures in your home.
16. Desserts made with raw eggs are safe if completely frozen before serving.

Answers

1. False

Symptoms of food poisoning usually start more than 24 hours after eating the contaminated food.

2. True

Avoid unpasteurized juice, especially for young children, the elderly, and anyone with a suppressed immune system.

3. False

Bacteria that cause food poisoning don't necessarily cause food spoilage, so they cannot be detected by the appearance or smell of the food.

4. False

Put hot leftover food into small shallow containers and promptly refrigerate. Otherwise the internal temperature can be high enough to allow bacteria to grow.

5. False

Never feed honey to infants less than 12 months old. Spores present in honey can cause botulism, an often fatal illness. The digestive tracts of older children and adults are resistant to the bacteria.

6. True

Raw meat or poultry may contain bacteria that could be spread to other foods. Plastic or glass cutting boards can be put in the dishwasher, washed with hot soapy water, or cleaned with a mixture of 1 teaspoon bleach to 1 quart of water. Don't reuse the cloth or sponge used to wipe up juices from raw meat. Launder them in hot soapy water before using them again. Paper towels should be thrown away right after they are used.

7. True

The surface of any raw food can be contaminated. Illness has been traced to cantaloupe, tomatoes, strawberries, scallions, alfalfa sprouts, and leaf lettuce. Always wash fresh produce in clear running water. Wash melons, squash and potatoes before cutting into them. Rinse and drain packaged vegetables and salad mixes.

8. False

Store eggs in the carton on a refrigerator shelf. Many refrigerator door egg trays do not stay cold enough to be safe.

9. False

Do not keep hard-boiled eggs at room temperature for more than two hours. Store them in the refrigerator and use within a week.

10. False

Thaw frozen foods in the refrigerator, or microwave and immediately cook them. Thawing at room temperature allows the outside of the food to reach dangerous temperatures even though the center of the food may remain frozen.

11. True

Foods kept frozen at 0°F or less are safe indefinitely. However, the flavor and quality will suffer and the food may get freezer burn.

12. True

The appearance of meat is not a foolproof test of doneness. Measuring the temperature of meat with a meat thermometer is the only way to assure that meat is safe to eat.

13. False

Most food-borne illness in this country occurs in private homes.

14. False

Each year millions of Americans suffer from food poisoning. There are thousands of severe cases and some fatalities. Many cases of food poisoning are wrongly assumed to be stomach flu.

15. True

Careful food handling, preparation, and storage can prevent most cases of food poisoning.

16. False

Freezing does not kill the salmonella bacteria so this is a risky practice. Try substituting pasteurized egg products in the recipe.

Your Food Safety I.Q.

How did you score? Give yourself 2 points for each correct answer.

26-32 Above Average—You are probably doing almost everything you can to prevent food-borne illness in your family.

20-24 Average—You may be taking some chances that could result in unpleasant consequences.

0-18 Below Average—You need to learn more about food safety and good food handling practices.

Food Poisoning Prevention Tips

Grocery shopping

- Don't buy cracked eggs. Cracks in eggshells can allow bacteria to get into the eggs.
- Don't buy unpasteurized milk, cheese, tofu, or fruit juices.
- Don't buy bulging, or damaged cans, torn packages, or outdated foods.
- Keep meat separated from other foods in your grocery cart or bag.
- When you have several errands to run, do your grocery shopping last.
- Refrigerate or freeze perishable foods as soon as you get home.

Food preparation

- Always wash your hands before preparing food.
- Wash the tops of cans with hot soapy water before opening them. Dirt and bacteria on the lids can be deposited in the food by the can opener blade.
- Herbed oils may have a risk of botulism due to botulism spores on the herbs. The acid in herbed vinegars prevents this problem.
- Cook egg dishes (French toast, omelets, etc.) until no liquid egg remains.
- Marinate meat in the refrigerator. Discard any extra marinade after it has been on raw meat.
- Always wash your hands and any other used surfaces with hot soapy water after handling raw meats.
- Don't cook large cuts of meat such as roasts or whole poultry in a slow cooker.

- Bake meat and casseroles containing meat and poultry at 325°F or higher.
- Cook ground meats thoroughly. Undercooked ground meat may cause e. coli poisoning in children.
- Reheat leftovers until they are steaming hot (165°F) to kill any bacteria that are present.

Food serving

- Keep cold foods cold and hot foods hot when serving buffet style.
- Don't allow *double dipping*. Instead, use separate serving utensils to spoon food onto individual plates.
- If you feed your baby directly from a baby food jar, don't save the left-overs. Enzymes from the baby's mouth cause the food to deteriorate allowing bacteria to grow in the food.
- Don't leave perishable food out of the refrigerator for more than two hours, one hour on hot days.
- Avoid serving acidic foods in ceramic, antique, or collectible containers. The containers may contain lead.

Food storage

- Test the temperature of your refrigerator with an appliance thermometer. It should be 40°F or lower. The freezer should be 0°F or lower.
- Foods that spoil quickly such as eggs and meats should not be stored on refrigerator door shelves. Most refrigerator door shelves are not cold enough. Use the door shelves for catsup, salad dressings and other bottled foods.
- Frozen food is safe indefinitely but the palatability will decrease over time.
- Before freezing, seal foods in plastic or aluminum wrap or freezer bags and write the date on the package.

- Keep raw refrigerated meats wrapped so their juices can't drip onto other foods.
- Place leftover food in the freezer if it will not be eaten in 3 to 4 days.
- **When in doubt, throw it out!**

Kitchen cleaning guidelines

- Replace cutting boards when they get cracks or grooves that are hard to clean.
- Wipe up spills on cupboard and refrigerator shelves immediately.
- Don't store food in undercounter cabinets through which water pipes run. Rodents may have easy access to these areas.
- Look through the refrigerator once a week and throw out perishable food.

Special food safety tips for children

- Teach children to wash their hands before eating. Have them sing the ABC song to time their hand washing.
- Don't allow children to lick serving utensils.
- Teach children not to eat food that has been left out of the refrigerator.
- Teach children how to recognize food that has spoiled.
- Don't allow children to play with a pet while eating as an animal's fur and saliva may carry harmful bacteria.
- Don't use plastic trays from packaged meat for children's craft projects.

Tips for a safe picnic

- Take wet towelettes for cleaning surfaces and hands, a cloth for the picnic table, and plenty of clean plates, cups, and utensils.
- When packing a cooler, fill extra space with ice or cold packs.
- Put beverages in a separate cooler, so if it is left open, perishable foods will not be exposed to warm air.
- Use a meat thermometer to judge the doneness of meat and poultry cooked on a grill.
- Grilled meat should not be put back on the plate used for raw meat.
- Keep hot foods hot and cold foods cold.
- Don't set the cooler in direct sunlight. Keep the lid closed as much as possible.
- Perishable foods can be dangerous in just one hour at summertime temperatures.

Drinking water safety guidelines

- Test well water at least once a year for bacteria and other contaminates.
- If lead solder was used on water pipes, have tap water tested for lead.
- Don't drink water from a stream, pond, lake, or pool.
- Sterilize water by boiling it for one or two minutes when mixing formula for an infant younger than 2 months of age.
- Bottled water is not necessarily sterile and should also be boiled for infants less than 2 months of age.
- For more information about drinking water safety, call your local county health department for information or call the EPA hotline at 1-800-426-4791.

Choking

Choking on food is a significant hazard for preschool children. Young children do not know how to chew well and don't really use a grinding chewing motion as adults do until they are about four years of age. Choking can be caused by food getting lodged in the esophagus and putting pressure on the airway or by food being inhaled directly into the windpipe. Foods that are hard and do not dissolve easily in saliva are the most dangerous.

Common causes of choking in children under the age of four

- Hot dogs
- Raw carrots and celery
- Peanut butter
- Hard candies—even jelly beans can be easily inhaled
- Popcorn
- Raisins
- Grapes
- Chunks of meat or other firm foods
- Nuts and seeds

Preventive measures

- Cut hotdogs lengthwise, then in slices.
- Steam vegetables lightly to make them softer and easier to chew.
- Spread peanut butter in a thin layer or mix with honey or jam.
- Cut grapes into slices.

- Teach children not to talk or laugh with food in their mouths.
- Don't allow children to run around with food in their mouths.
- Don't force food on children or try to rush them to eat as that may cause gagging and choking.
- Watch that children don't stuff too much in their mouths at once.
- Be cautious about allowing toddlers to eat in the car, especially if there is not another adult to assist if they choke.
- Make sure foods are in a size and texture your child can handle.
- Never leave a child unsupervised while eating. Listening from the next room is not good enough as a choking child may not be able to make any noise.
- Teething products that numb the gums should not be used before a feeding as they can numb the throat and interfere with swallowing ability.
- Always have your child in an upright position when feeding.
- Make sure that older children know not to give a younger one a dangerous food.
- Don't give preschoolers hard candies, tough meats, stringy foods, or nuts and seeds.
- Children who have prematurity, hypotonia (poor muscle tone), cerebral palsy, or developmental delays, may have swallowing disorders. Talk to your pediatrician about doing a swallowing study.
- Take a first aid class and learn CPR.

Kitchen Safety

The kitchen is probably the most dangerous room in your house. Children can have access to sharp objects, hot objects, electric appliances, and other hazards. Look at your kitchen from the standpoint of your young child. What is within reach? If your child is a climber, what can be reached by climbing on furniture?

Here are some other things to consider:

- Be sure food heated in the microwave is stirred well. Microwaves often heat food unevenly, leaving hot spots.
- Infants have been seriously burned by formula heated in a microwave. Always thoroughly shake liquids after heating and check the temperature before feeding them to your child.
- Don't use disposable plastic baby bottle liners in microwave ovens as the liners can burst.
- Preschool children should never operate a microwave oven or other appliance.
- Don't hold a child in your arms when cooking or when removing food from a microwave or oven.
- Use the back burners when possible so your child can not reach hot pans. Turn the pan handles to the rear of the stove.
- Don't allow infants or young children to play underfoot when you are cooking. Keep your child in a highchair or playpen instead.
- Keep appliances unplugged when not in use.
- When using electric crockpots, frying pans, coffee pots, etc. be sure children can not reach the cords and pull the appliance off the counter.
- Always keep knives and other sharp objects out of the reach of children.
- Make sure your water heater is set no higher than 120°F to avoid burns.
- Keep cleaning supplies, medications, and other toxic substances out of reach or locked up.
- Don't leave young children unsupervised in the kitchen.
- Don't hold a baby or young child on your lap while you are drinking a hot liquid.

Growth Charts

How to Use Growth Charts

Plotting a child's height, weight, and head circumference on a growth chart is an important part of a well-child exam. There are several purposes for growth charts:

- Compare a child's length to that of other children of the same age.
- Compare a child's weight to that of other children of the same age.
- Compare a child's head circumference to that of other children of the same age.
- Compare a child's body mass index to that of other children of the same age.
- Follow a child's growth over time.

The comparison of a child's growth with other children of the same age and gender is given in percentiles. For example, if a child's height is at the 75th percentile that means that out of 100 typical children 25 would be taller than the child and 75 would be the same height or shorter.

A child's growth pattern should be tracked over a period of time. One measurement may be misleading if a child is just starting into a growth spurt or is in a temporary slowdown. If a child who has been at the 50th percentile falls to the 25th percentile the cause could be an illness or nutritional problem, or just a genetic pattern that the child is following. When interpreting a child's percentiles it is helpful to know the parent's heights and whether they were early, average, or late to develop. The charts do not tell you what is ideal, only what is typical. It may be perfectly healthy for a child with short parents to be at the 5th percentile for height and weight.

In May 2000 the Center for Disease Control released the first new growth charts since 1977. They contain more accurate information and are appropriate for all ethnic groups. For the first time there are charts to assess BMI or body mass index, the relationship of weight to height. These can help identify children who are becoming overweight or underweight.

On the following pages you will find growth charts for children from birth to 20 years. The charts printed here are weight for age, height for age, and head circumference for age. There are BMI charts for ages 2 to 20. To use the charts find the chart for your child's age and gender. Plot your child's measurements on the appropriate charts. If your child is between two and three years of age and the height measurement is taken with the child standing use the 2 to 20 year chart. If the height measurement is taken with the child lying down use the 0 to 36 month chart. If you have any concerns about your child's percentiles consult your pediatrician.

Directions for calculating BMI and percentiles

Body mass index or BMI measures the relationship of weight to height. By calculating your child's body mass index and plotting it on a chart you can determine whether your child is becoming overweight or underweight. Be sure your child has been weighed and measured accurately. Using measurements made on home equipment may not be reliable enough to draw any conclusions. To calculate body mass index use one of the following formulas:

English formula:

[weight in pounds ÷ height in inches ÷ height in inches] X 703 = BMI

Metric formula:

[weight in kilograms ÷ height in meters ÷ height in meters] = BMI

Or find your child's BMI by using the BMI calculator on the Center for Disease Control website at:

http://www.cdc.gov/nccdphp/dnpa/bmi/calc-bmi.htm.

When you have the BMI number plot it on the body mass index-for-age charts on the following pages and find the percentile for your child's BMI. There are charts for girls and for boys.

What the BMI percentile means:

- 95th percentile or higher is considered overweight.
- 85th percentile–95th percentile is at risk for becoming overweight.
- Under the 5th percentile is considered underweight.

If you have any concerns about your child's percentiles consult your pediatrician.

CDC Growth Charts: United States

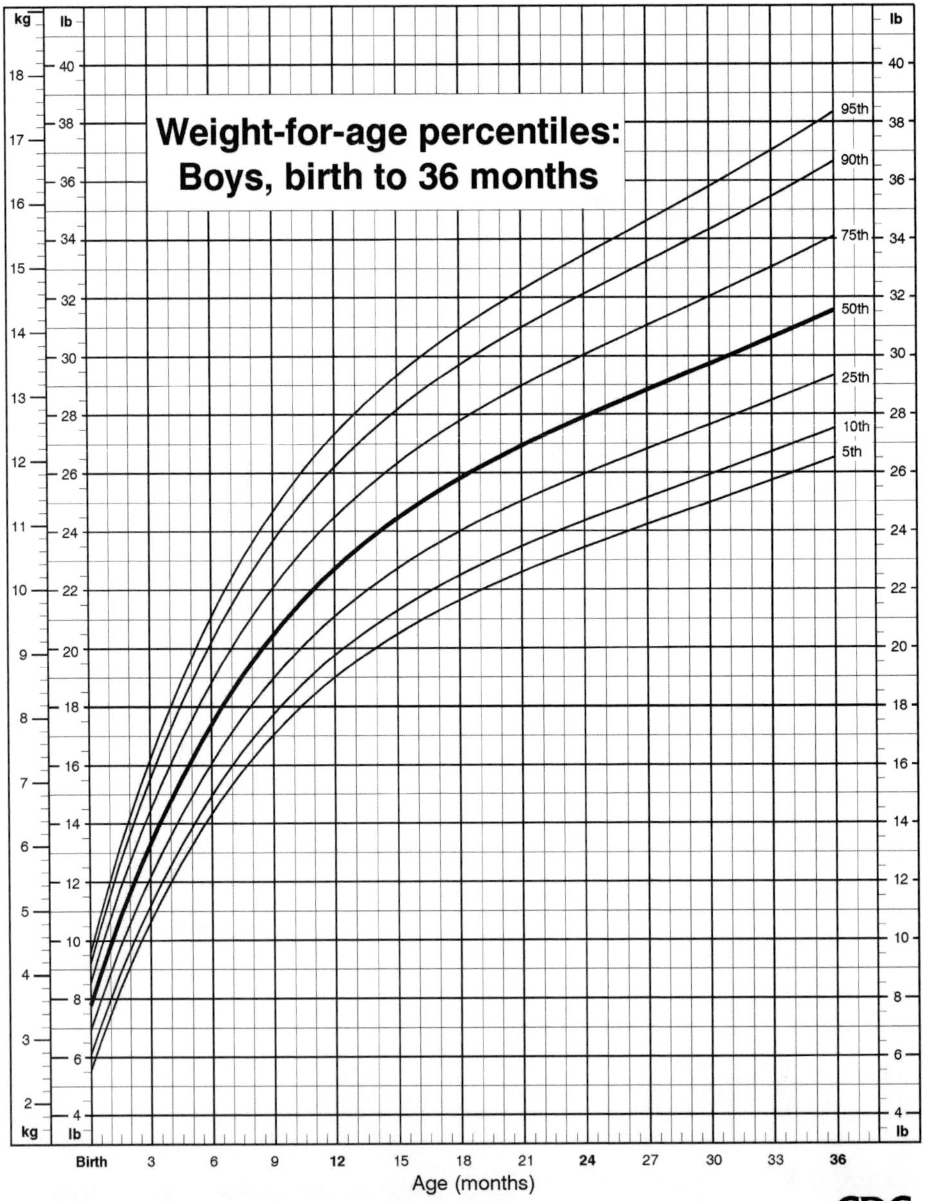

SOURCE: Developed by the National Center for Health Statistics in collaboration with
the National Center for Chronic Disease Prevention and Health Promotion (2000).

CDC
CENTERS FOR DISEASE CONTROL AND PREVENTION

CDC Growth Charts: United States

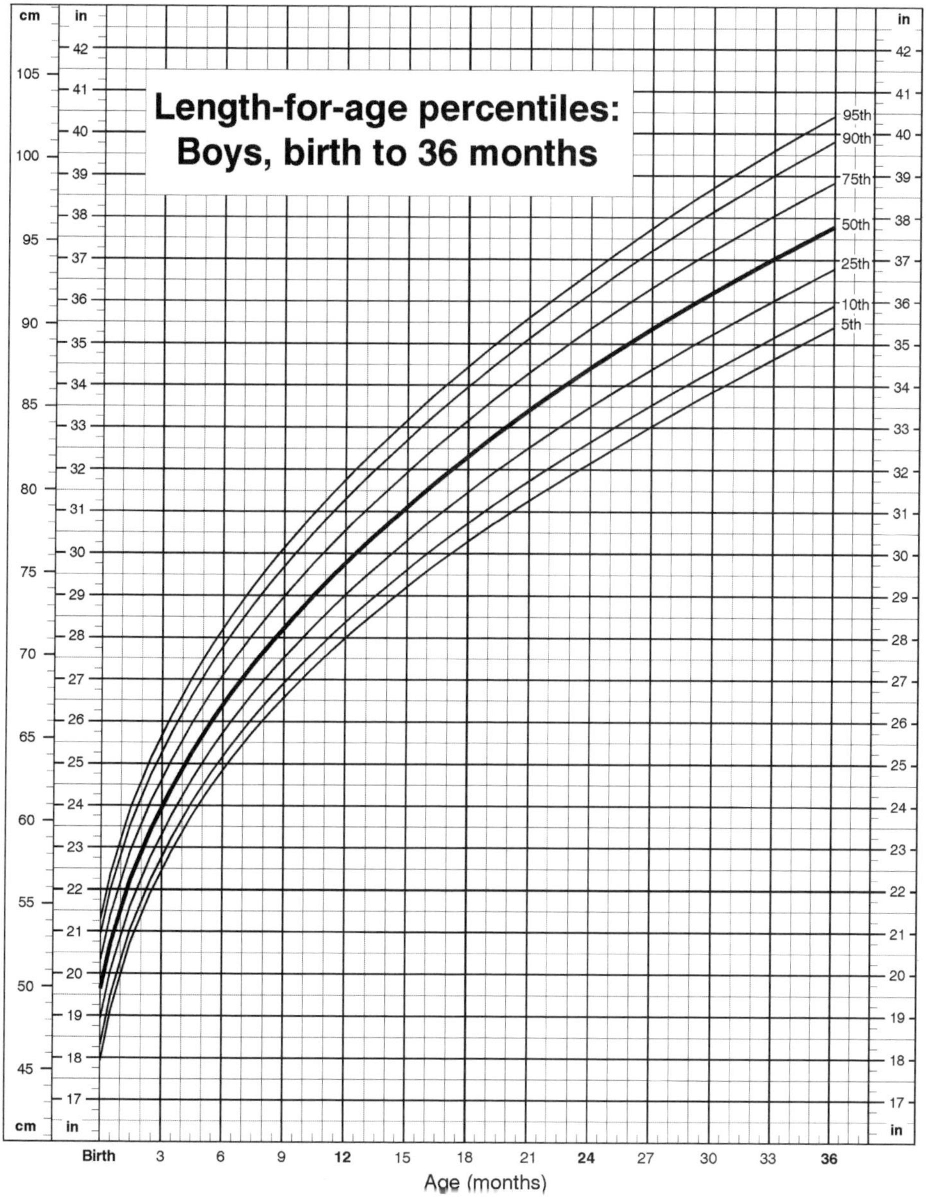

SOURCE: Developed by the National Center for Health Statistics in collaboration with the National Center for Chronic Disease Prevention and Health Promotion (2000).

CDC Growth Charts: United States

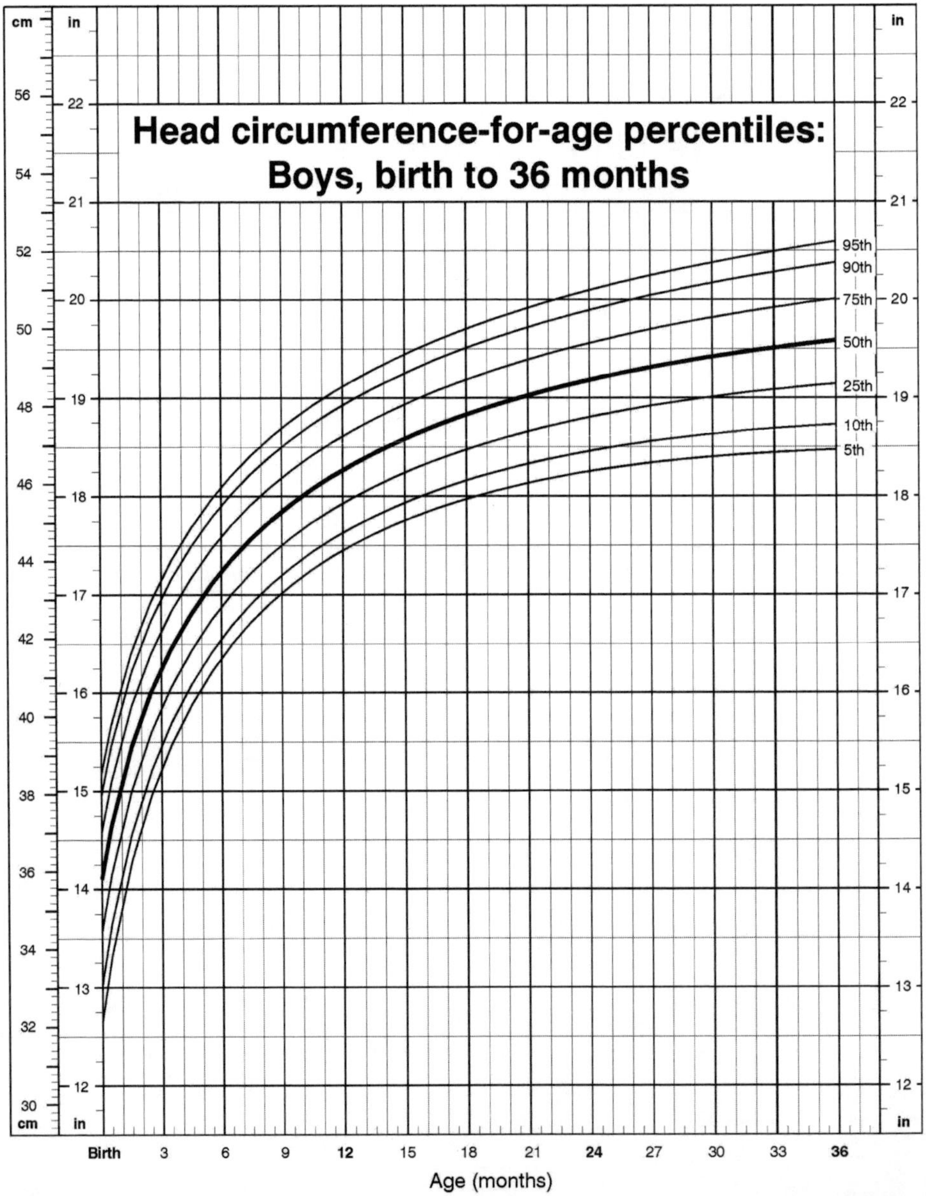

SOURCE: Developed by the National Center for Health Statistics in collaboration with the National Center for Chronic Disease Prevention and Health Promotion (2000).

CDC Growth Charts: United States

**Weight-for-age percentiles:
Boys, 2 to 20 years**

Age (years)

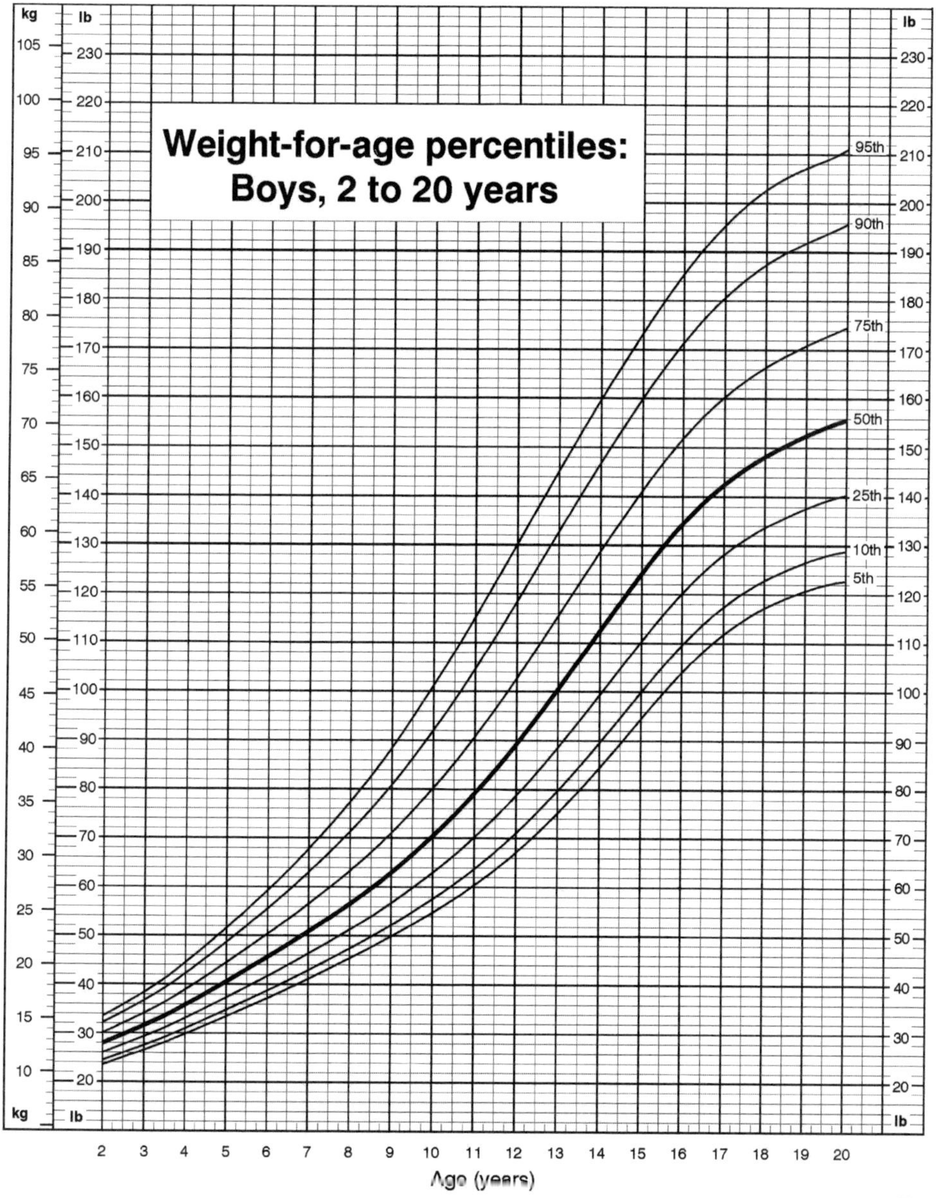

SOURCE: Developed by the National Center for Health Statistics in collaboration with
the National Center for Chronic Disease Prevention and Health Promotion (2000).

CDC Growth Charts: United States

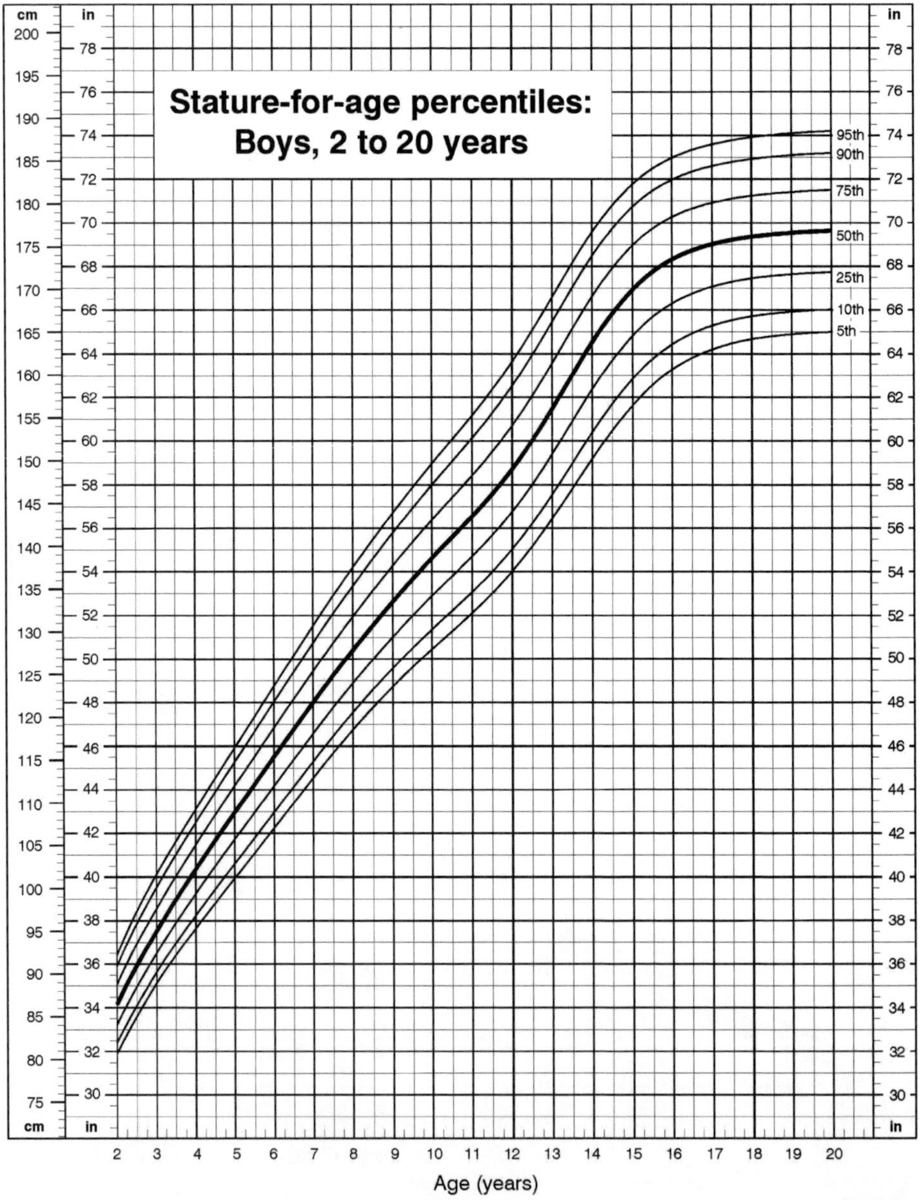

SOURCE: Developed by the National Center for Health Statistics in collaboration with
the National Center for Chronic Disease Prevention and Health Promotion (2000).

CDC

CDC Growth Charts: United States

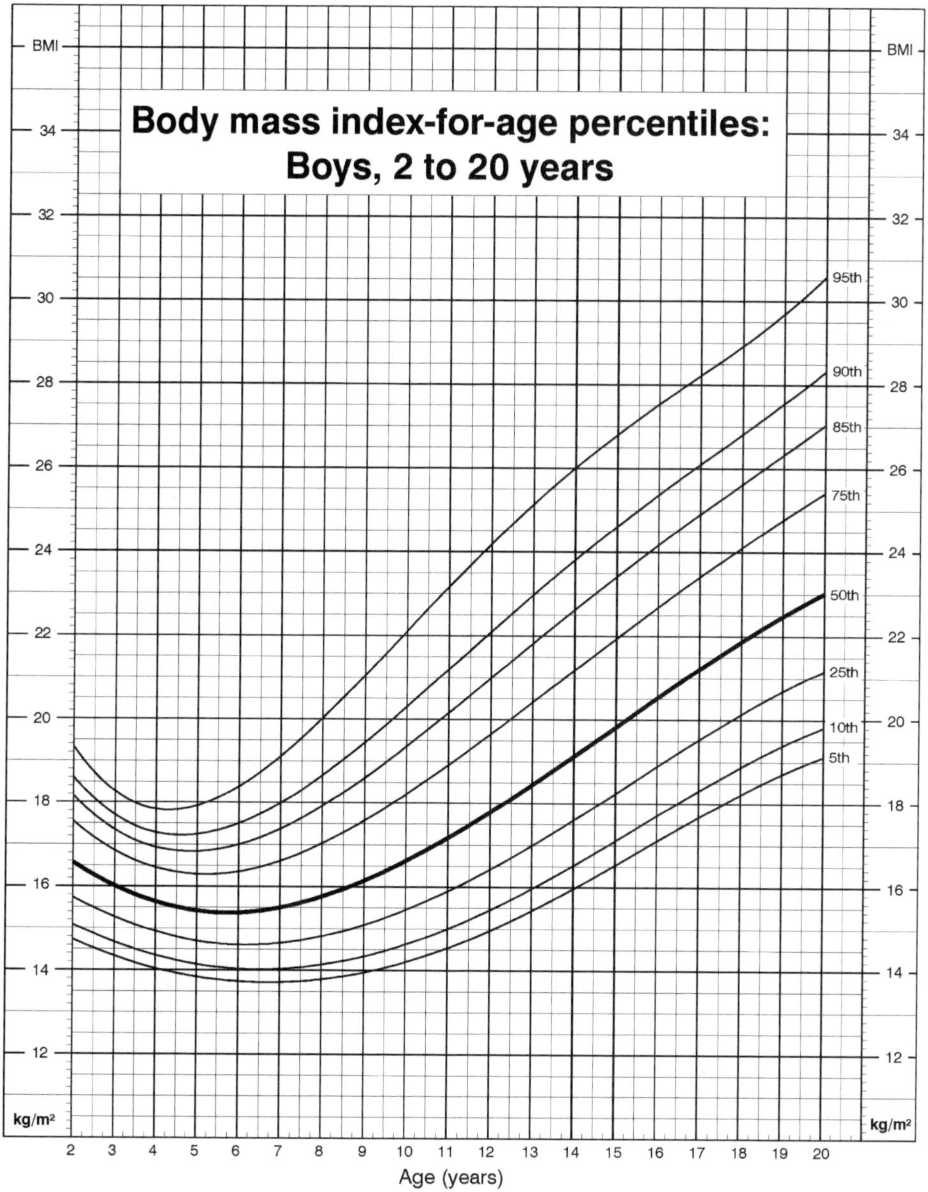

SOURCE: Developed by the National Center for Health Statistics in collaboration with the National Center for Chronic Disease Prevention and Health Promotion (2000).

CDC

CDC Growth Charts: United States

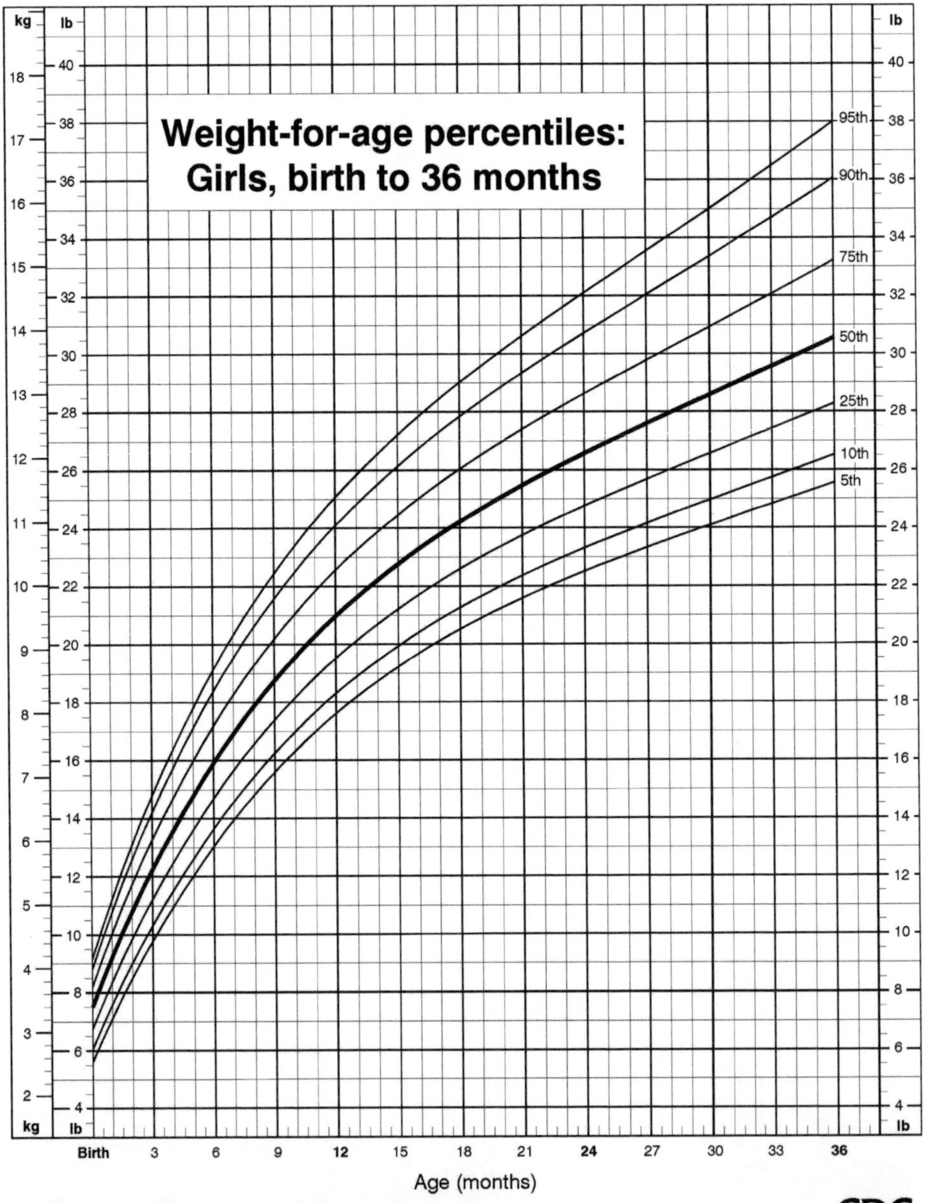

SOURCE: Developed by the National Center for Health Statistics in collaboration with the National Center for Chronic Disease Prevention and Health Promotion (2000).

CDC Growth Charts: United States

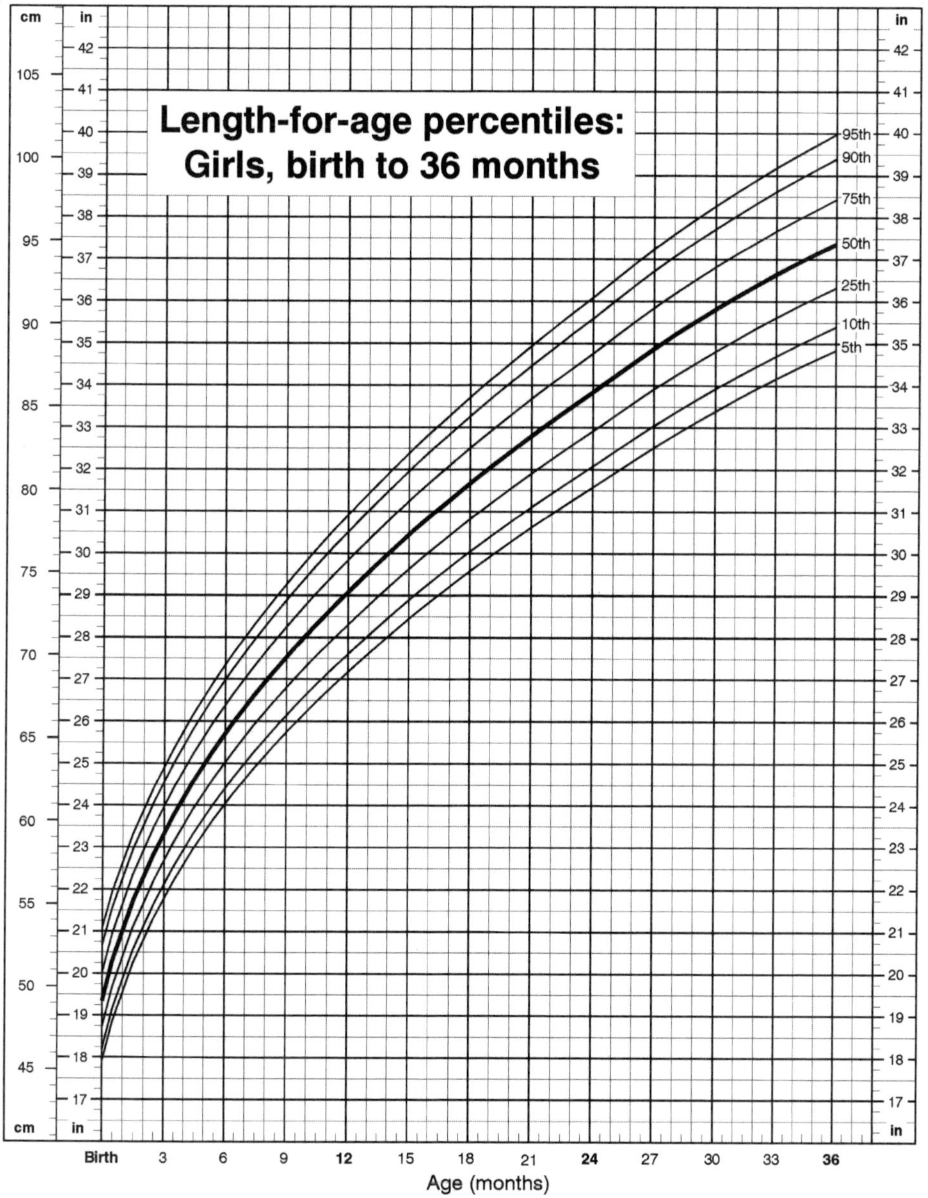

SOURCE: Developed by the National Center for Health Statistics in collaboration with the National Center for Chronic Disease Prevention and Health Promotion (2000).

CDC Growth Charts: United States

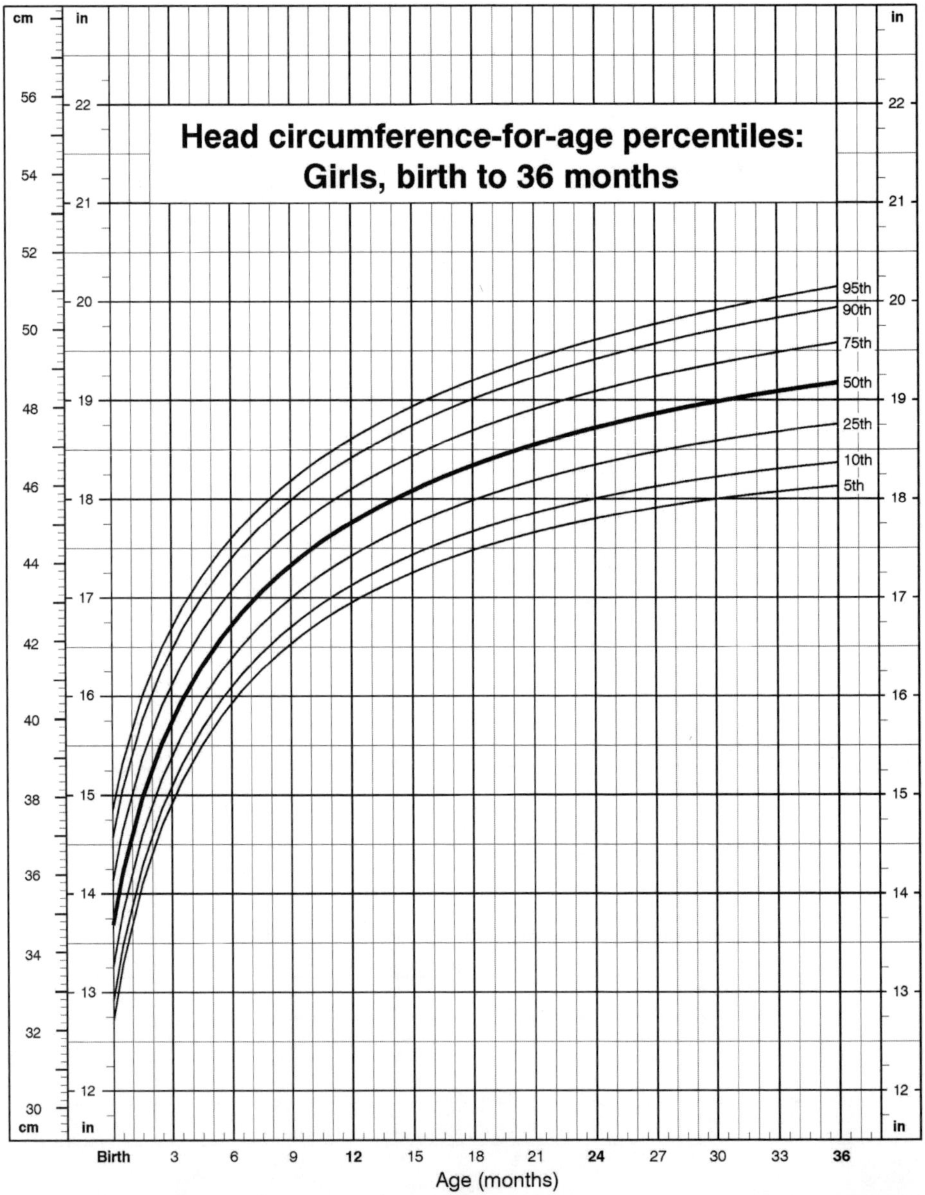

SOURCE: Developed by the National Center for Health Statistics in collaboration with the National Center for Chronic Disease Prevention and Health Promotion (2000).

CDC

CDC Growth Charts: United States

**Weight-for-age percentiles:
Girls, 2 to 20 years**

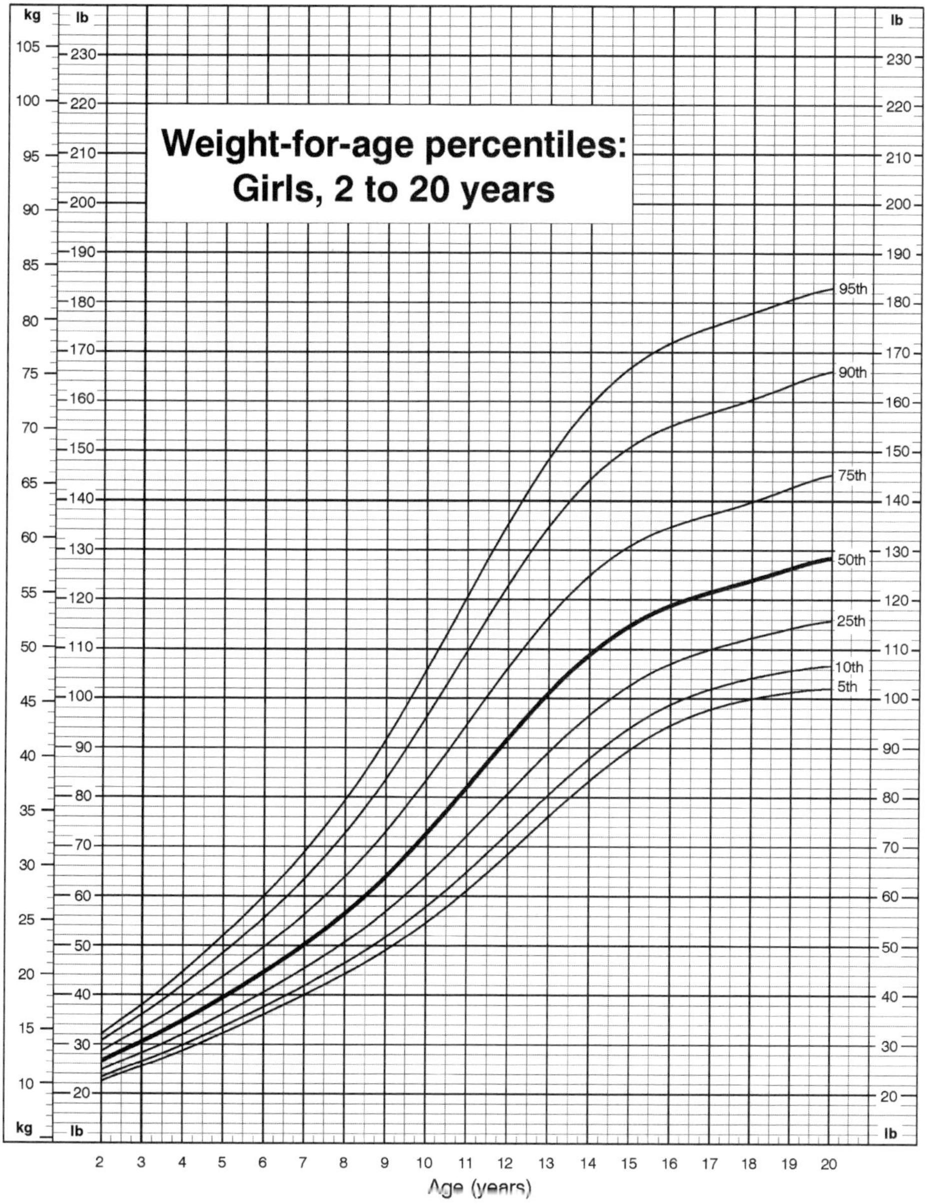

SOURCE: Developed by the National Center for Health Statistics in collaboration with
the National Center for Chronic Disease Prevention and Health Promotion (2000).

CDC Growth Charts: United States

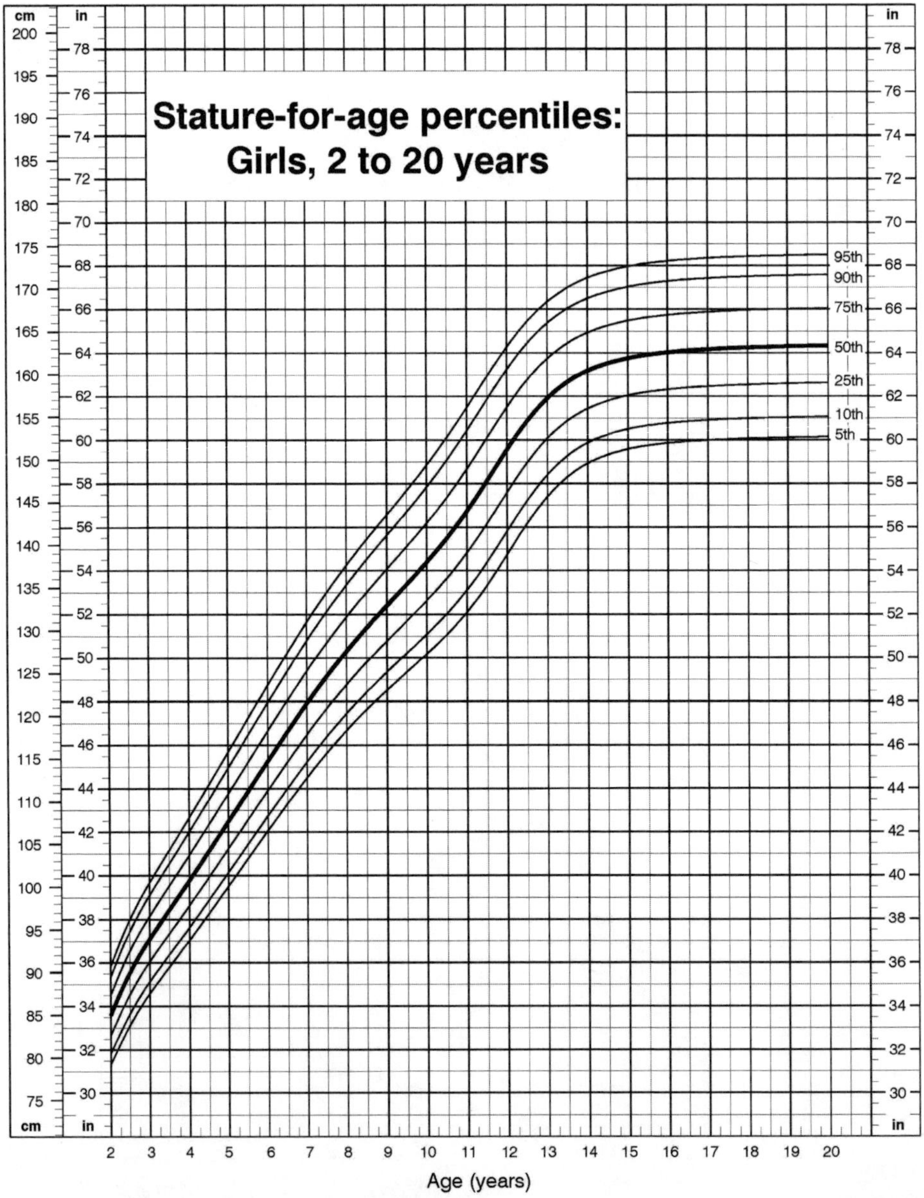

SOURCE: Developed by the National Center for Health Statistics in collaboration with the National Center for Chronic Disease Prevention and Health Promotion (2000).

CDC Growth Charts: United States

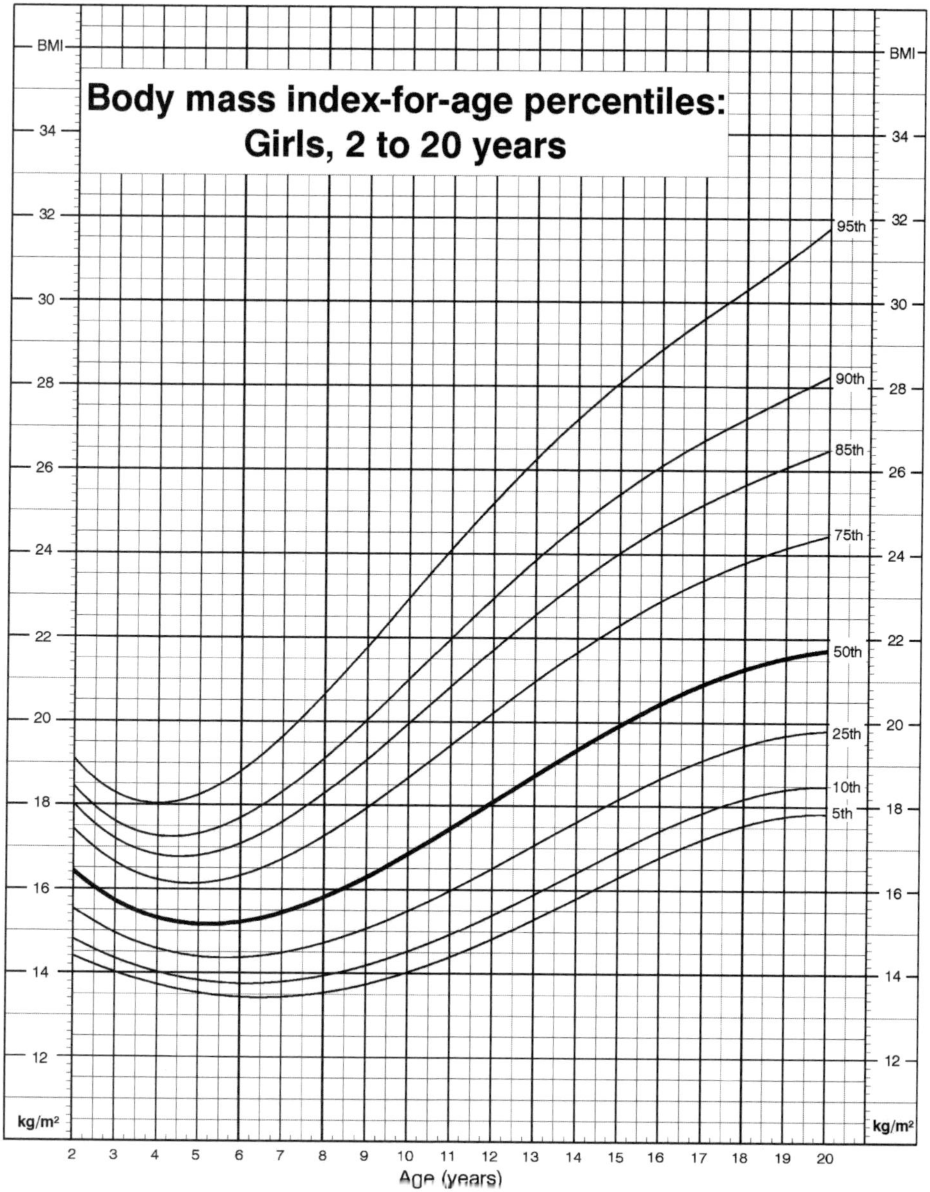

SOURCE: Developed by the National Center for Health Statistics in collaboration with the National Center for Chronic Disease Prevention and Health Promotion (2000).

CDC

Resources

We read dozens of books and articles and visited many websites while preparing this book. Here are the ones we think are the most helpful for those who want more information. Because we know that feeding your little one is only one of the many concerns you may have we have included some of our other favorite parenting resources.

Books and Other Publications

Kids General Health

Eisenberg, Arlene, Heidi E. Murkoff, and Sandee E. Hathaway. *What to Expect the Toddler Years*. Workman Publishing Co., 1996.

Written by the same authors as *What to Expect when You're Expecting* and *What to Expect the First Year*, this comprehensive guide answers parent's questions about toddlers. It covers things such as toilet learning, tantrums, sleeping and feeding problems, keeping children safe and much more.

Schiff, Donald, Steven P. Shelov, editors. *American Academy of Pediatrics Guide to Your Child's Symptoms: The Official, Complete Home Reference, Birth Through Adolescence*. Villard Books, 1997.

This is an excellent reference book. Helps you quickly assess your child's symptoms and determine when you can safely handle them at home, and when you need to call the pediatrician. You will save time and money and avoid unnecessary doctor visits. Easy to use. Highly recommended.

Shelov, Stephen P., Robert E. Hannemann, and Catherine D. DeAngelis, editors. American Academy of Pediatrics, *Caring for Your Baby and Young Child: Birth to Age Five.* Bantam Doubleday Dell, 1998.

The first half of the book covers month-by-month descriptions of development, nutrition, and information about caring for your child from infancy to five years of age. The second half contains what you need to know about handling childhood emergencies as well as more routine childhood illnesses. Behavioral issues are covered as well.

Weissbluth, Marc. *Healthy Sleep Habits, Happy Child.* Fawcett Books, 1999.

Having trouble getting your little one to sleep well? This is the book for you. Read it and you will learn how to help your baby or preschooler develop better sleep habits. The information is based on good research and really works.

Wolf, Cindy. *On the Safe Side*. Whirlwind Publishing, 1998.

On the Safe Side is a complete guide to recognizing and correcting the hazards in a child's environment. The book takes you on a virtual walk-through of your home, pointing out the possible dangers and what to do about them. Full of practical and accurate advice, *On the Safe Side* should be required reading for all new parents.

Nutrition

Dietz, William and Lorraine Stern, editors. *American Academy of Pediatrics Guide to Your Child's Nutrition*. Villard Books, 1999.

An authoritative guide to developing healthy eating habits, written by the national organization for pediatricians. This is a good basic nutrition book. Covers birth through adolescence.

Satter, Ellyn. *How to Get Your Kid to Eat, But Not Too Much.* Bull Publishing Company, 1987.

This is a classic resource book about children's eating habits. Shows how to help your child develop healthy eating patterns from birth through adolescence. If you are continuing to struggle with difficult eating behaviors this book can help.

Satter, Ellyn. *Secrets of Feeding a Healthy Family*. Kelcy Press, 1999.

The latest book by Ellyn Satter extends her advice about eating well to adults. It includes recipes, tips on grocery shopping, meal planning, and kitchen utensils.

Tamborlane, William V., editor. *The Yale Guide to Children's Nutrition*. Yale University Press, 1997.

For the parent who wants more extensive nutrition information. This book covers nutrition from infancy to adolescence including chapters on medical conditions that require special diets. More information than most will need.

Websites

Any printed list of websites may soon be out of date. Visit our site, http://www.foodfortots.com for a current list.

Kid's General Health

http://www.aap.org

Official site for the American Academy of Pediatrics, the national professional organization for pediatricians. A reliable source of information about children's health.

http://www.healthykids.com

Healthy Kids magazine's web page. Chat rooms for parents of children of all ages. Also up-to-date health information.

http://www.imsafe.com

Good child safety site with product recall information and a free newsletter.

http://www.twinsmagazine.com

Site for Twins Magazine. Lots of information about twins. Fun to visit even if you aren't the parent of twins.

Nutrition

http://www.eatright.org/finddiet.html

American Dietetic Association site. Find a registered dietitian in your area. The site also has good information, games for older children, daily tips.

http://www.foodfortots.com

Companion site for this book. Visit often to keep up with new information and sign-up for a free email newsletter by sending an email to list@foodfortots.com.

http://www.ificinfo.health.org

International Food Information Council. Translates nutrition research into understandable and useful articles for the public. Covers a wide range of nutrition topics.

http://www.lalecheleague.org

Official site of the La Leche League. Information about breastfeeding. There is even a contact form to ask for help with a breastfeeding problem from an accredited La Leche League leader.

http://www.mayohealth.org

Do you have questions about vegetarian diets? Read the articles on this site from the Mayo Clinic. Find them by clicking on their Nutrition link. Other good health information too.

http://www.navigator.tufts.edu

Tufts University Nutrition Navigator. Comprehensive guide to nutrition resources on the Internet. They score websites according to the value of the content. A good source if you want to do in depth reading about nutrition.

http://www.nutrition.cornell.edu/nutriquest

Nutriquest site, sponsored by Cornell University. Questions and answers to common nutrition questions. You can send in your questions to be answered by their staff.

http://www.nutritionforkids.com

24 Carrot Press and Connie Evers, the author of *How to Teach Nutrition to Kids,* operate this nifty site. There is a newsletter archived on the site and ordering information for books and materials about how to teach nutrition information to children.

http://www.tinytummies.com

Sanna James, MS, RD edits this site. Pediatric nutrition information and research, recipes, and practical ideas for parents and professionals. Subscribe to TinyTummies newsletter.

http://www.usda.gov/news/usdakids/

Loads of information about nutrition including the food pyramid for young children. You can even print off a copy.

Food Safety

http://www.cfsan.fda.gov

Consumer advice from the Food & Drug Administration Center for Food Safety and Applied Nutrition. Topics covered include food safety, food handling and preparation, nutrition and weight loss, and food labels.

http://www.fightbac.org

Fight Bac site of the Partnership for Food Safety Education. The place to go if you want more information about food poisoning. Lots of good practical information on how to feed your family safely.

http://www.fsis.usda.gov

USDA Food Safety and Inspection Service. There is also a toll-free 24 hour USDA Meat and Poultry hotline: 1-800-535-4555 with recorded messages about food safety. During office hours experts are available to answer questions.

Drinking Water

http://www.epa.gov/safewater

U.S. Environmental Protection Agency Office of Ground Water & Drinking Water. Check to see if any problems have been reported with your local water system. Also information about lead in drinking water. Or you can call the EPA Safe Drinking Water Hotline at 1-800-426-4791.

Eating Disorders

http://www.aabainc.org

The American Anorexia/Bulimia Association web site. Information about eating disorders. What to do if you suspect that you or a loved one suffers from one of these disorders. Reviews of books on the subject also.

Food Allergies

http://www.aaaai.org

Official website for the American Academy of Allergy, Asthma & Immunology. Authoritative information about allergies, including food allergies.

http://www.aanma.org

Allergy and Asthma Network/Mothers of Asthmatics site. For a donation you can subscribe to the

MA report, containing updates about food allergy, and allergy and asthma products. Ask the allergist column and more.

http://www.foodallergy.org

This is an important resource for authoritative information about food allergies. Updated constantly with information about ingredients in commercially prepared food. Particularly helpful for those with serious or life-threatening food allergies.

Special Conditions

http://www.childrenwithdiabetes.com

Information and resources for parents of diabetic children.

http://www.jdf.org

The Juvenile Diabetes Foundation, an excellent source of information and resources for parents who have a child with this condition.

http://www.sinetwork.org

Sensory Integration Resource Network. Information about this disorder which may cause poor feeding due to extreme sensitivity to textures and tastes, physical awkwardness, and learning difficulties.

Index

A

Allergies,
- anaphylaxis, 245–246
- cow's milk, 169–170
- food, 245–247
- hives, 245
- soy milk, 170

anemia, iron deficiency, 197
antibiotics and meat, 198
apple(s), applesauce, see also fruit,
- Apple Crisp Muffins, 32
- Applesauce Gel Squares, 86
- Caramel Apple Dip, 136
- Cinnamon-Applesauce Ornaments, 145
- Fruit Leather, 88
- Fruit Mini Pies, 118
- Fruit Salad, 95
- Graham Cracker Applesauce Dessert, 115
- Grilled Cheese & Apple Sandwiches, 49
- Puffy Apple Pancake, 62

B

Baby food,
- commercial, 174
- homemade, 173–174
- foods to avoid in first year, 178–179
- quantity to feed, 173, 180–181
- resistance to spoon feeding, 176
- starting, 171–172, 247
- tongue thrust reflex, and, 171

Baby's First Cake, 146
Baby's First Cookie, 103
Baked Fries, 75
Baked Potato Bar, 61
Baking Soda Volcanoes, 162
banana, see also fruit,
- Banana Cookies, 99
- Banana Cupcakes, 104
- Banana French Toast, 41
- Banana Frosting, 105
- Banana Pops, 85
- Cherry Banana Smoothie, 24
- Easy Banana Cream Dessert, 116
- Fruit Salad, 95
- Orange Banana Milk, 19
- Peanut Butter, Banana, & Jam Minimuffins, 34
- Peanut Butter Banana Smoothie, 22

Beans, Calico, 73
Birdseed Pinecones, 159
birthday party ideas, 149
body mass index,
- obesity, and, 227
- calculating percentiles, 260

bottle feeding, see formula,
botulism, and honey, 178, 249
bran, see fiber, grains
Bran, Refrigerator Muffins, 35
BRAT diet, and gastroenteritis, 241
bread, see also muffins, pancakes,
- Cheezy Pretzels, 112
- Eggnog Bread, 139
- Ten-Day Squish Bread, 124

Breakfast Burritos, 43
Breakfast Casserole, Make-Ahead, 39
breastfeeding,
- after one year of age, 210
- alcohol, and, 179
- allergies, and, 170, 246
- benefits to mother and baby, 169
- colic, and, 170, 244
- mother's diet, and, 169–170, 246

Broccoli Salad, 74
Bubbles, 157
Butter, 114
Burritos, Breakfast, 43

C

Caffeine, see also carbonated beverages,
- breastfeeding, and, 179
- effects of, 179, 198

cakes, cupcakes,
- Baby's First Cake, 146
- Banana Cupcakes, 104
- Fruit & Cereal Breakfast Cake, 36
- Fruit Cocktail Cake, 98
- Ice Cream Cone Cakes, 147
- Krazy Kake, 126
- Sweetheart Cupcakes, 132

calcium, see dairy products, minerals
Calico Beans, 73
calories, 186
Caramel Apple Dip, 136
carbohydrates, see also grains, sugar,
  calorie content of, 186
  complex vs. simple, 192
carbonated beverages, see also caffeine,
  avoiding, 212
  inappropriate for infants, 178
  nutritional value, 193
carotenemia, 188
carrots, see also vegetables,
  Baby's First Cake, 146
  Baby's First Cookie, 103
  Orange Glazed Carrots, 76
  White Grape & Carrot juice, 25
celiac sprue, 245
Celery, Magic Colored, 161
cereal, see also grains,
  Fruit & Cereal Breakfast Cake, 36
  Muesli, 38
  infant's diet, and, 171, 180–181
cheese, see also dairy products,
  Cheezy Pretzels, 112
  Easy Cheese Sauce, 77
  Grilled Cheese & Apple Sandwiches, 49
  Mac'n'Cheese, 56
  Yogurt Cheese, 81
Cherry Banana Smoothie, 24
Chicken Haystacks, 66
Chicken Nuggets, 64
Chicken Parmesan, 67
Chicken Turtles, 65
chocolate,
  Chocolate Dipped Fruit, 131
  Confetti Sticks, 148
  Krazy Kake, 126
  No-Bake Cookies, 119
  Peanut Butter Chocolate Chip Cookies, 102
  inappropriate for infants, 179
choking,
  causes, 220, 221, 233, 255
  infants, and,176, 178
  prevention, 255–256
cholesterol, 194
Cinnamon-Applesauce Ornaments, 145
colds, see upper respiratory infections
colic, 243–245
constipation, see also fiber, 242–243
Confetti Sticks, 148
cookies,
  Baby's First Cookie, 103
  Banana Cookies, 99
  High Fiber Cookies, 101
  No-Bake Cookies, 119
  Oatmeal Cookies, 100
  Peanut Butter Bars, 106
  Peanut Butter Chocolate Chip Cookies, 102
  Pumpkin-Packed Cookies, 137
  Sour Cream Sugar Cookies, 120
cow's milk, see milk
Crackers, Vegetable, 111
Cream Cheese Frosting, 133
Crepes, 42
cup, introducing, 175
cupcakes, see cakes

D

Dairy products, see specific dairy products, calcium,
  food pyramid guidelines, 189
  picky eater tips for, 189
dehydration and gastroenteritis, 241
diarrhea, 241–242
dips,
  Caramel Apple Dip, 136
  Dilly Dip, 91
  Fruit Dip, 90
  Peanut Butter Dip, 89
Donut Muffins, 29
Dough Ornaments, 144

E

E. coli, see also food poisoning, 252
Eating disorders, 223–226
egg(s) and egg dishes,
  Banana French Toast, 41
  Breakfast Burritos, 43
  Colored Eggs, 135
  Crepes, 42

Egg Salad Sandwiches, 48
Eggnog Bread, 139
Make-Ahead Breakfast Casserole, 39
Omelets, 40
Perfect Hardboiled Eggs, 134
Puffy Apple Pancake, 62
allergy, and, 178, 246
safe storage of, 249
Salmonella risk, 250
English Muffin Pizzas, 51
exercise, 225, 230

F

Fats and oils, 190–191, 193–194
fever, 238–239
fiber, see also grains,
Fruit & Cereal Breakfast Cake, 36
High Fiber Cookies, 101
Muesli 38
Oatmeal Cookies, 100
Prune Muffins, 31
Refrigerator Bran Muffins, 35
Vegetable Crackers, 111
Whole Grain Pancakes, 37
constipation, and, 197, 242–243
dietary guidelines, 194–195
finger foods, 176–179
Fizzy Fruit Juice, 20
fluoride, 170, 196, 201
food additives, 198–199
food allergies, see allergies
food group pyramid, 185
food poisoning, see also e. coli, 247–253
formula,
colic, and, 244
microwave heating, 257
iron and vitamin content, 170–171
milk allergy, and, 169–170
sterilizing water for, 170, 254
tooth decay, and, 218
weaning, 179, 210, 217–218
French Toast, Banana, 41
Fries, Baked, 75
frostings,
Banana Frosting, 105
Cream Cheese Frosting, 133
Peanut Butter Frosting, 107
Pudding Frosting, 127
Frozen Yogurt, Easy, 97
Frozen Yogurt Sandwiches, 83
fructose intolerance, 188
fruit(s), see also specific fruits,
food pyramid guidelines, 188
infant's diet, and, 180–181
Fruit & Cereal Breakfast Cake, 36
Fruit Cocktail Cake, 98
Fruit Dip, 90
fruit juices,
Fizzy Fruit Juice, 20
Fruity Juice, 21
Grape Milk, 19
Ice Cube Tray Popsicles, 123
Strawberry Lemonade, 22
Tummy Warming Cider, 20
White Grape & Carrot Juice, 25
constipation, and, 242
diarrhea, and, 188
infants, and, 175, 180–181
limiting, 210, 219
nursing bottle tooth decay, and, 218
unpasteurized risky, 178, 247–248
Fruit Leather, 88
Fruit Mini Pies, 118
Fruit Pizza, 122
Fruit Prints, 157
Fruit Salad, 95
Fruity Jigglers, 87
Fudgesicles, Striped, 84

G

Gastroenteritis, 239–242
genetic engineering of food, 198–199
Gingerbread House, 140
Glop, 154
Glue, 156
goat's milk, 178
Graham Cracker Applesauce Dessert, 115
grains, see also fiber,
food group pyramid guidelines, 186–187
Grape Milk, 19
Grilled Cheese & Apple Sandwiches, 49
growth, see also growth charts, weight,

family patterns, 222
slowing in second year of life, 205, 211
vegetarian diet, and, 191–192
growth charts, 259–273

H
Hawaiian Muffins, 53
herbal remedies, avoid for children, 197, 238, 244
High Fiber Cookies, 101
hives and food allergy, see allergies
honey and botulism risk, 178, 249

I
Ice Cream Cone Cakes, 147
infant foods, see baby food
iron, see also minerals,
cow's milk, and, 189
function and sources, 197, 201
infants, and, 171
vegetarian diet, and, 191
irradiation of food, benefits, 198

J
Juices, see fruit juices
junk food, 210, 212, 221

K
Krazy Kake, 126

L
Lactose intolerance, 169, 245

M
Mac'n'Cheese, 56
Magic Colored Celery, 161
Make-Ahead Breakfast Casserole, 39
meals,
behavior at, 205–207, 213–214, 218, 231
timing of, 210, 214–215
meat(s) and other protein, see also specific meats,
Chicken Haystacks, 66
Chicken Nuggets, 64
Chicken Parmesan, 67
Chicken Turtles, 65
Make-Ahead Breakfast Casserole, 39
Mexican Stackups, 68
Mixer Meatloaf, 70
Sneaky Joes, 72
food pyramid guidelines, 190
function and sources, 195
infant's diets, and, 180–181
picky eater tips for, 190
safe handling of, 249–250
Meatloaf, Mixer, 70
Mexican Stackups, 68
microwave safety, 257
milk, cow's, see also dairy products, formula,
Grape Milk, 19
Orange Banana Milk, 19
Orange Cooler, 21
Peanut Butter Banana Smoothie, 22
allergy to, 245–246
anemia, and, 197
colds, and, 237
food pyramid guidelines, 189
hormones in, 199
infants, and, 169, 175, 178
introducing to toddler's diet, 179
lactose intolerance, 245
picky eater tips for, 189, 219–220
unpasteurized risky, 178, 199
minerals, see also fluoride, iron, 201
Mixer Meatloaf, 70
Muesli, 38
muffins,
Apple Crisp Muffins, 32
Donut Muffins, 29
Hawaiian Muffins, 53
Peanut Butter, Banana, & Jam Minimuffins, 34
Prune Muffins, 31
Refrigerator Bran Muffins, 35
Sweet potato Muffins, 30

N
Natural foods, 174, 199
No-Bake Cookies, 119
No-Bake Pumpkin Pie, 138

O
Oat(s), oatmeal,
Apple Crisp Muffins, 32
High Fiber Cookies, 101
Muesli, 38
Oatmeal Cookies, 100
Peanut Butter & Jam Minimuffins, 34
Vegetable Crackers, 111

obesity, see weight
Omelets, 40
Orange Banana Milk, 19
Orange Cooler, 21
Orange Glazed Carrots, 76
organic foods, 199–200
ornaments, Christmas tree,
Cinnamon-Applesauce Ornaments, 145
Dough Ornaments, 144
overweight, see weight

P

Pancakes,
Puffy Apple Pancake, 62
Whole Grain Pancakes, 37
pasta,
Mac'n'Cheese, 56
Rainbow Pasta, 158
Twisty Pasta Salad, 52
peanut butter,
Banana Pops, 85
No-Bake Cookies, 119
PB&J Mini Pies, 54
Peanut Butter Chocolate Chip Cookies, 102
Peanut Butter, Banana & Jam Minimuffins, 34
Peanut Butter Banana Smoothie, 22
Peanut Butter Bars, 106
Peanut Butter Dip, 89
Peanut Butter Frosting, 107
allergy to, 246
choking hazard, 178
Pears, Poached, 96
Peek-A-Boo Pockets, 55
picky eaters,
age characteristics, 205–207
dinner, and, 212–214
fruits, and, 188
meat and, 190
milk, and, 189, 219–220
new foods, and, 213–214
one bite rule, and, 214, 219
vegetables, and, 187, 218–219
pie,
Fruit Mini Pies, 118
PB&J Mini Pies, 54
No-Bake Pumpkin Pie, 138
pineapple, see also fruit,
Fruit Pizza, 122
Fruity Juice, 21
Hawaiian Muffins, 53
Pineapple Slush, 82
Piña Colada, Easy, 24
Pinecones, Birdseed, 159
pizza,
English Muffin Pizzas, 51
Fruit Pizza, 122
Peek-A-Boo Pockets, 55
Playdough, Super Scented, 153
Poached Pears, 96
Popsicles, Ice Cube Tray, 127
potato, see also vegetable,
Baked Fries, 75
Baked Potato Bar, 61
pretzels, see also grains,
Cheezy Pretzels, 112
Confetti Sticks, 148
protein, see meat and other proteins
Prune Muffins, 31
Pudding Frosting, 127
Puffy Apple Pancake, 62
Pumpkin-Packed Cookies, 137
Pumpkin Pie, No-Bake, 138

R

Rainbow Pasta, 158
Refrigerator Bran Muffins, 35
restaurant meals, 232–234
Rubber Flub, 155

S

Salads,
Broccoli Salad, 74
Fruit Salad, 95
Twisty Pasta Salad, 52
salmonella, see food poisoning
sandwiches,
Egg Salad Sandwiches, 48
Grilled Cheese & Apple Sandwiches, 49
PB&J Mini Pies, 54
Peek-A-Boo Pockets, 55
Sneaky Joes, 72

Tortilla Rollups, 47
Tuna Burgers, 57
Sauce, Easy Cheese, 77
serving sizes for preschoolers, 186, 211
sneaking food, 221–222
Sneaky Joes, 72
soft drinks, see carbonated beverages
solid foods, see baby food
Sour Cream Sugar Cookies, 120
sourdough, Ten-Day Squish Bread, 124
soy milk,
allergy,170
inappropriate for infants, 178
stomach flu, 239–242
strained food, see baby food
strawberry, see also fruit,
Easy Frozen Yogurt, 97
Fruit Pizza, 122
Strawberry Lemonade, 22
Tutti-Frutti Smoothie, 23
Striped Fudgesicles, 84
sugar,
behavioral effects of, 191
cereals, 210
Sugar Cookies, Sour Cream, 120
Sugar Cube Buildings, 160
supplements, 196–197
Super Scented Playdough, 153
Sweet Potato Muffins, 30
sweeteners, artificial, 198
Sweetheart Cupcakes, 132

T
Tasting Game, 163
Ten-Day Squish Bread, 124
tooth decay, see also fluoride, 218
tortilla(s), see also grains,
Breakfast Burritos, 43
Tortilla Bowls, 69
Tortilla Rollups, 47
Zucchini Quesadillas, 50
Tummy Warming Cider, 20
Tuna Burgers, 57
Tutti-Frutti Smoothie, 23
Twisty Pasta Salad, 52

U
Upper respiratory infections, 237–238

V
Vegetable(s), see also specific vegetables,
food pyramid guidelines, 187
infant diet, and, 180–181
picky eater tips for, 187, 218–219
safe preparation of, 249
Vegetable Crackers, 111
vegetarian diet, 170, 191–192, 197
vitamins,
dietary guidelines chart, 202
infants, and, 170–171, 180–181
supplements, 197, 238
types, 196
Volcanoes, Baking Soda, 162
vomiting, 240–241

W
Water,
encouraging intake of, 222–223
fluoridation, 171, 196
heater temperature, 257
infants, and, 170, 180–181
intoxication, 240
safe drinking water, 254
sterilization for bottles, 170, 254
weaning, from bottle or breast, 179, 210, 217–218
weight,
attitude about, 224–226
body mass index, and, 227, 260–261
overweight, 226–230
underweight, 222
Whole Grain Pancakes, 37

Y
Yogurt, see also dairy products,
Cherry Banana Smoothie, 24
Easy Frozen Yogurt, 97
Easy Piña Colada, 24
Frozen Yogurt Sandwiches, 83
Fruit Dip, 90
Peanut Butter Dip, 89
Striped Fudgesicles, 84
Tutti-Frutti Smoothie, 23
Yogurt Cheese, 81

Z
Zucchini Quesadillas, 5

About the Authors

Dr. Janice Woolley and Jennifer Pugmire are a mother-daughter team who coauthored Food for Tots.

Dr. Janice Woolley is a pediatrician with more than twenty years experience providing medical care to children. Over the years she has helped parents with their concerns about providing healthy food for their preschool children. As a result of this experience, she recognized the need for an up-to-date cookbook for parents. Dr. Woolley is a graduate of Brigham Young University and Indiana University School of Medicine and received her training in pediatrics at the University of Washington. She practices pediatrics in the greater Seattle area and was chosen by a survey of her peers as one of Seattle's Best Doctors for two consecutive years. She is the mother of four children, and grandmother of four preschoolers.

Jennifer Pugmire graduated cum laude from Brigham Young University in statistics and math. Currently the stay-at-home mom of three young children, she has also taught in a co-op preschool. She has been leader of a church nursery for children aged 18 months to 3 years and has done home day care for preschoolers. She has hands-on experience with the challenge of feeding toddlers nutritious foods.

ORDER FORM FOR FOOD FOR TOTS™

Great gifts for new parents, grandparents, daycare providers, church nursery leaders and others. Satisfaction guaranteed. Perfect fundraiser for organizations!

Order today—choose one:

- Call our toll-free number: **1-866-foodfortots**—please have your credit card ready
- Place your order through our secure Internet site: **http://www.foodfortots.com**
- Fill in the order blank below, enclose payment and mail to:

Food for Tots
Division of Mammoth Media
P.O. Box 241
Mercer Island, WA 98040-0241

Order with friends and save money on shipping and handling fees.

Send me ______ **Books @ $16.95** each **Subtotal** _______

Shipping & Handling$4.00 first book, **$2.00** each additional book _______

WA residents only:

add **$1.84** sales tax first book, **$1.76** each additional book _______

Total _______

Payment method:

Check or Money Order payable to **Food for Tots** for __________ is enclosed.

Please charge my ____ VISA _____ MasterCard

Canadian orders must be accompanied by money order in U.S. funds or credit card order.

Name ______________________________ email __________________

Address ____________________________________ Phone __________

City ________________________________ State _____Zip __________

Card #____________________________________Exp. Date __________

Card Holders Signature ____

__**Send me information about your special quantity discounts for fundraisers**

Please allow 15 days for delivery